For the people ensuring that the future we automate remains worthy of trust.

"The future is already here; it's just not evenly distributed."
— William Gibson

WHY MOST DATA PROJECTS FAIL

Designing for Success in the Age of AI

BIJO JOSE

AUTUMNLEAF PRESS

Washington, DC

Why Most Data Projects Fail: Designing for Success in the Age of AI

Published by AutumnLeaf Press
The Data & AI Expert Series

Paperback ISBN 978-1-971193-00-7
Hardback ISBN 978-1-971193-01-4
Ebook ISBN 978-1-971193-02-1

Printed in the United States of America

Cover design by AMR studio
Interior design by AutumnLeaf Press

First Edition

Library of Congress Control Number: 2026933947

Table of Contents

Preface

We live in a world saturated with data. Yet behind all that motion, I have heard the same quiet truth for most of my career: many data projects still fail. Not for lack of tools. Not for lack of talent. But because meaning is the first thing to disappear when speed becomes the goal.

Across federal healthcare, financial systems, and large enterprise transformations, I have watched brilliant teams deliver immaculate pipelines, only to return to spreadsheets because no one trusted the numbers. I have seen organizations adopt modern architectures while admitting, almost softly, that they still do not know what their data means.

Those moments stayed with me. They shaped how I design and how I lead. They taught me that data is not simply a technical artifact. It is a form of understanding. And trust does not emerge from platforms. It is built when people share the same language, the same intent, and the same definitions.

This book comes from more than two decades of living inside those lessons. I have seen projects rise when meaning is clear, and I have seen them quietly collapse when it is not. I have learned that progress is not always faster movement. Sometimes it is deeper thinking. Semantics, governance, and clarity are not bureaucracy. They are the foundations that make truth durable.

If there is one message I hope you carry with you, it is this:

Data does not fail. Design does.

And the future, especially the AI powered future, belongs not to those who collect the most data, but to those who understand it best.

– Bijo Jose

CHAPTER 1

The Data Illusion: Motion Is Not Meaning

"Where is the wisdom we have lost in knowledge?
Where is the knowledge we have lost in information?"
— T.S. Eliot

Framing the Illusion

Every age has its illusion of progress.

Ours is the illusion that *data itself* will save us.

Across industries and continents, organizations chase the promise of becoming "data-driven." Executives speak of data as the new oil, the new electricity, the new competitive edge. Transformation roadmaps are drawn. Platforms are procured. Teams are built. And everywhere, the same narrative unfolds: more data means more value.

Cloud vendors promise infinite scale. Dashboards multiply faster than the insights they claim to deliver. Machine-learning algorithms whisper predictions from oceans of noise. New titles—Data Evangelist, Chief Data Officer, AI Strategist—appear in org charts as emblems of modernity. The message seems clear: if you can measure it, you can master it.

But beneath this glittering progress, something quieter is breaking down. The more we collect, the less we seem to understand.

We've built the pipelines but not the purpose. We've automated processes without agreeing on what they mean. Data flows faster than ever, but clarity moves slower than before.

The tools evolve; the trust erodes.

And yet, the illusion persists because motion feels like mastery. When dashboards light up, pipelines hum, and metrics climb, it creates a sense of control. Movement masquerades as maturity. But what we call progress is often just activity amplified by automation.

We are not suffering from a scarcity of data; we are drowning in abundance without alignment.

Organizations have become factories of measurement.

Success is tallied not in shared understanding but in statistics:

- Number of dashboards launched.
- Terabytes processed per day.
- Models deployed to production.
- LLM usage and AI agents shipped.

These are comforting metrics; easy to report, easy to celebrate. But they measure motion, not meaning. They tell us how fast we are moving, not whether we're heading in the right direction.

Behind the scenes, conversations about *governance* or *definitions* are treated as tedious obstacles to "real progress." Leaders urge teams to "move faster," unaware that acceleration without alignment magnifies confusion. Every tool added to an ungoverned system increases entropy. The paradox of modern data work is that the more sophisticated our infrastructure becomes, the easier it is to hide misunderstanding beneath it.

A thousand pipelines can now distribute data instantly but if each one carries a slightly different definition of "customer" or "order" or "outcome," all we've done is accelerate disagreement.

The Illusion of Progress

The CEO leaned forward during the quarterly review.

"Quick question," she asked. "How many active customers do we have?"

Three heads turned to three different dashboards. Three numbers. All correct. None aligned.

One team had defined "active" as any email click in 30 days. Another used repeat purchases. A third relied on revenue thresholds.

Silence followed. Then confusion. Then blame.

That moment unraveled months of work and exposed the fragility beneath the company's sophisticated data stack. Despite a modern stack of petabytes, pipelines, polished dashboards, and AI agents meaning was absent. This is the data fallacy: the illusion that infrastructure equals insight.

We celebrate speed and scale. But clarity, the most vital element, is missing. Motion is not meaning. Sophistication is not maturity.

Until we realign our focus from infrastructure to semantics, from tooling to trust, we will continue to chase the illusion of progress.

Four Layers of Maturity

As we explore this illusion, it's helpful to anchor ourselves in a simple framework. These four layers capture the progressive stages of a healthy data ecosystem, and how fragility often stems from skipping steps:

1. Motion – This is the visible, energetic layer. It includes infrastructure rollouts, pipelines, dashboards, and tooling. Organizations at this level focus on doing more: ingesting data, deploying platforms, and automating workflows. But motion alone says nothing about accuracy, alignment, or usability. It looks impressive but often operates in isolation from real decision-making needs.

2. Clarity – This is the semantic layer. It means terms are defined, concepts agreed upon, and metrics consistently interpreted across teams. Clarity requires coordination, governance, and negotiation. It's often invisible to outsiders but absolutely foundational. Without clarity, every dashboard becomes a debate and every meeting a reconciliation exercise.

3. Trust – The behavioral layer. This is when stakeholders rely on the data to make decisions with confidence. It shows up in fewer contested meetings, faster decision cycles, and KPIs that are debated for their meaning, not their math. Trust requires both semantic alignment and cultural reinforcement. It's a lagging indicator of clarity and a leading indicator of insight.

Most data failures stem from confusing activity for alignment, from assuming that Layer 1 (Motion) automatically leads to Layer 3 (Trust). It doesn't. You can have dashboards without decisions, pipelines without purpose, and tools without trust.

4. Insight – This is the outcome layer. When motion, clarity, and trust converge, organizations gain the ability to act with precision and confidence. Insight isn't just having more data or fancier reports. It's using trusted, shared, and timely information to drive impactful decisions. This is the point where the data stops being an asset on paper and becomes a strategic advantage in practice.

Maturity isn't how many tools you deploy. It's how confidently your people can use the data to act. As you climb from Motion to Insight, ensure every AI component is contract-bound (Clarity), relied on (Trust), and proves outcome lift (Insight).

Data Maturity Progression

Stage	Characteristics	Risks if neglected
Motion	Activity, tooling, pipelines	Vanity metrics, false urgency
Clarity	Defined terms, shared understanding	Dashboard debates, semantic drift
Trust	Stewardship, consistency, usability	Audit failures, loss of confidence
Insight	Actionable, aligned, meaningful data	Strategic missteps, insight gaps

Each layer builds upon the one before. Without clarity, trust collapses. Without trust, insight evaporates.

AI makes dashboards brighter but misalignment louder. Let's examine the signals and move from illusion to practice

Part 1: False Signals of Maturity

Mirage in the Metrics

In an era of AI, big data, and cloud-native tools, it's easy to mistake tooling for transformation. Dashboards flourish. Pipelines scale. AI models churn. But beneath the gloss, leaders question basic metrics. Teams reconcile reports. Conflicting numbers derail decisions.

Why? Because tooling progress often masks semantic regression.

Sophistication dazzles. But understanding stalls. Inconsistent definitions. Missing lineage. Contradictory dashboards. These are symptoms of misalignment not misconfiguration.

The Hospital Analogy: Sophisticated Tools, Fragmented Care

Imagine walking into a state-of-the-art hospital. The halls gleam with cutting-edge equipment: robotic surgery units, AI-driven triage systems, and real-time biometric dashboards. From the outside, it's a marvel of modern healthcare.

But inside, dysfunction rules.

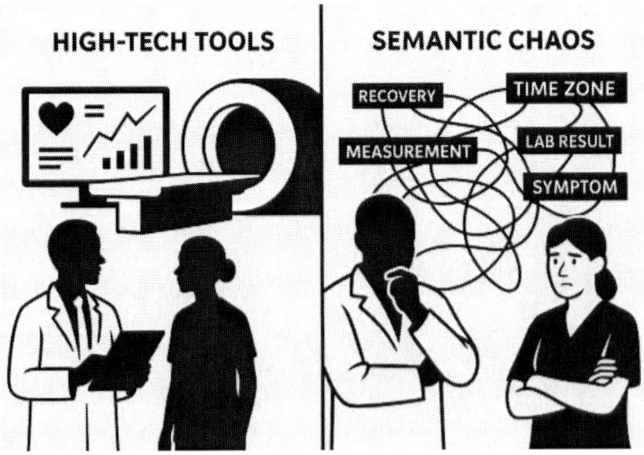

Figure 1.1 High-tech tools with underlying semantic chaos.

Cardiology and oncology departments use incompatible electronic health record systems. Recovery is defined differently depending on the specialty. Lab results are stored in varying formats and units. Nurses document care using shorthand that physicians don't understand. Specialists operate in information silos, each assuming they're aligned when they're not.

The consequences are real: delayed diagnoses, redundant testing, conflicting prescriptions, and eroded trust between care teams. The infrastructure is advanced, but without coordination, the system falters.

This is what it's like to build a data ecosystem without semantic alignment. You can have world-class data warehouses and sleek dashboards, but if definitions, ownership, and context are missing, you've built a high-tech maze. One where insight is possible in theory, but elusive in practice.

Just like the goal of a hospital isn't to collect vitals but to heal, the goal of a data platform isn't to store information, it's to create understanding. Without shared meaning, even the most powerful tools can fail the people they're meant to serve. Dashboards, data lakes, and AI models appear to indicate progress. But true maturity lies beneath:

As we'll explore throughout this book, the journey from motion to meaning unfolds across four progressive layers of data maturity: *Motion, Clarity, Trust,* and *Insight.* These layers define how organizations evolve from building pipelines to building understanding.

The Iceberg Illusion

At first glance, organizations appear to be making tremendous progress. Dashboards launch weekly, data lakes ingest terabytes by the hour, and AI models generate real-time predictions. But beneath this surface-level motion lie the structural weaknesses that ultimately determine whether data becomes an asset or an obstacle.

Think of an iceberg: visible activity above the surface, but unseen structures below. Dashboards, data lakes, and AI models appear to indicate progress. But true maturity lies beneath:

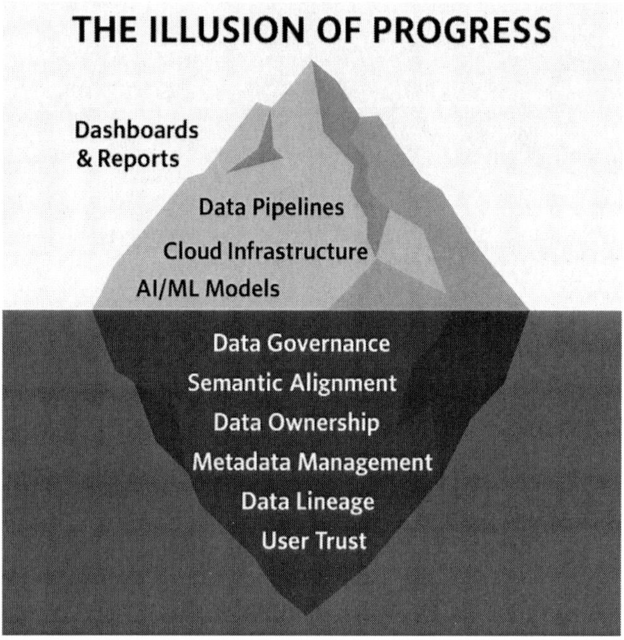

Figure 1.2 The illusion of progress: visible dashboards vs. hidden foundations of data trust.

Above Surface (Illusion)	**Below Surface (Foundation)**
Dashboards that dazzle but mislead	Terminological alignment
Moving Pipelines don't clarify	Ownership and stewardship
Models that infer without context	Metadata and lineage
Activity that looks like progress	Stakeholder trust

Until we address the submerged complexity, the iceberg will tip.

Many modernization programs mistake activity for progress. When pipelines multiply and dashboards proliferate, the illusion of maturity becomes self-reinforcing. Teams measure throughput instead of truth. In such environments, success is often defined by motion metrics — dashboards deployed, terabytes processed — while meaning remains undefined.

The following example illustrates how a well-funded modernization effort, built on impressive infrastructure, can still fail when semantics and ownership are absent.

Case Study: The $20M Government Mirage

A U.S. federal agency undertook a high-profile data modernization initiative, armed with $20 million in funding, bipartisan political support, and a goal to unify reporting across dozens of fragmented systems. The plan sounded promising: build a cloud-native data lake, integrate real-time dashboards, and deploy automated pipelines that would enable executives to make decisions at the speed of data.

The agency selected top-tier technology vendors. Consulting partners were brought in to architect pipelines, configure metadata catalogs, and manage cloud infrastructure. Dashboards began rolling out to key departments within the first year. Internally, the effort was seen as a model for digital transformation.

But cracks appeared almost immediately:

- **Definitions Conflicted**: What constituted a "closed case" varied from one division to another. One team counted any case assigned to a reviewer; another required audit sign-off. Even common metrics like "active participant" or "successful referral" lacked consensus.
- **Dashboards Went Unused**: Executives found the new dashboards impressive but untrustworthy. In some instances, numbers

contradicted reports prepared manually just days earlier. Over time, users returned to Excel for reports they could trust.

- **Data Ownership Was Absent**: An internal audit found that 42% of critical datasets had no named owner. Data lineage was murky. Catalog tools existed but were incomplete or poorly maintained.
- **Reversion to Manual Workflows**: Analysts, unable to trace how metrics were derived, stopped using the curated layers and relied on raw exports and legacy reports.

The turning point came when an oversight committee requested a cross-agency roll-up of key performance indicators. The request, which should have taken hours, triggered weeks of emergency reconciliation. Teams scrambled to retroactively align definitions, clean data sets, and explain contradictory results.

The result? The agency missed its reporting deadline, triggering public scrutiny and a formal investigation.

"We built the pipes," one senior director noted, "but forgot to agree on what should flow through them."

In response, a "Data Governance and Stewardship Council" was formed. Their first actions: identify owners for every strategic dataset, standardize critical definitions, and implement stewardship review cycles before publishing dashboards. Progress resumed but trust was already weakened.

This story illustrates more than a failed implementation. It reveals the deeper danger of building infrastructure without alignment. Semantics aren't an afterthought; they're the foundation. Without shared definitions and clear ownership, even a $20M system will amplify confusion rather than deliver clarity.

Part 2: The Tooling Trap

Across industries, data initiatives increasingly showcase high-tech deliverables as symbols of success: cloud migrations completed ahead of schedule, data lakes capable of ingesting petabytes daily, real-time dashboards glowing on executive iPads. These milestones are touted in quarterly reviews and strategy decks as hallmarks of maturity.

But what often goes unspoken is the creeping unease underneath.

Despite impressive activity, basic questions remain unresolved. Leaders ask for "customer lifetime value" and get five different answers. Data scientists build machine learning models, only to find business users don't trust the predictions. Analysts reverse-engineer pipelines to understand the numbers behind the charts they're supposed to interpret.

What's happening?

Technology without understanding only scales confusion.

This is the Tooling Trap: the false sense of maturity created by the presence of modern tools, regardless of their alignment with business logic, user needs, or semantic consistency. It's the dangerous belief that infrastructure inherently produces intelligence, or that more tools will automatically solve strategic problems.

In the next sections, we unpack the most common patterns of this trap and how to spot them before they ossify into organizational dysfunction.

Infrastructure ≠ Insight

Too often, organizations parade infrastructure milestones as evidence of transformation: "100 dashboards launched," "50TB migrated," or "machine learning integrated into our fraud detection flow." These metrics impress on slide decks and annual reports. But they are indicators of activity, not of alignment.

The real test is not how much data is moved, but how much of it is trusted. It is not how many dashboards exist, but how many are actually used in making decisions. When stakeholders cannot agree on definitions or outcomes, even the most elegant infrastructure becomes a house of mirrors reflecting confusion, not clarity.

The problem isn't the tools; it's the absence of a shared semantic foundation beneath them. Without alignment on core terms, context, and ownership, infrastructure only automates ambiguity.

Tools Without Purpose

Tool adoption without clear intent is one of the costliest mistakes in data programs. Platforms are procured because they are market leaders or because competitors have adopted them; not because they solve a specific, validated problem.

This leads to:

- **Shelfware**: Sophisticated tools that go unused after launch because teams lack time, training, or use cases.
- **Metric Sprawl**: Dashboards built without consensus on definitions become confusing or misleading.
- **Silo Reinforcement**: New tools intended to unify workflows often create parallel universes of logic and reporting.

Technology becomes ornamental; a veneer of progress that masks a lack of strategy. In such environments, even basic tasks like identifying a reliable sales metric become Herculean.

Before introducing any new tool, leaders should ask: *Who will use this? What decisions will it improve? How will we measure its value?* Without those answers, the tool becomes noise.

Data as Afterthought

Data is often treated as a secondary concern in software projects, something that can be retrofitted after applications are delivered. Business logic is hardcoded into microservices. Event tracking is scattered across logs. Data schemas evolve to meet system performance needs, not to reflect business meaning.

This creates an archaeological challenge for analysts. They are forced to:

- Interpret cryptic column names like cust_seg_lvl_3
- Guess the business logic behind transformations
- Build fragile queries that depend on undocumented behaviors

Documentation, if it exists at all, trails implementation by months. Domain knowledge lives in the heads of engineers or gets buried in long-abandoned project wikis. The result? Analysts spend more time decoding intent than delivering insights.

Until data is treated as a design asset from the start—modeled, documented, and governed in tandem with systems—data maturity will remain a mirage.

Performance Becomes Performative

In many organizations, data work becomes a performance, a show of activity designed to imply insight. Teams are celebrated for the number of dashboards created, not the decisions improved. Metrics are gamified, visualizations are polished, and daily standups echo with KPIs that no one fully trusts.

Meetings center around defending numbers rather than exploring actions. Disagreements about definitions are seen as political rather than strategic. Questioning a metric's source or meaning is perceived as a threat to progress.

In this environment, data culture becomes defensive. Learning stops. Feedback loops close. And decisions, though data-driven in appearance, drift further from reality. This is what performative data maturity looks like: motion without meaning, polish without precision, and confidence without coherence.

Part 3: Fragility in Practice

Even when organizations move fast, hire top talent, and adopt cutting-edge tools, they are not immune to breakdowns in meaning. In fact, rapid scaling often magnifies hidden inconsistencies. Fragility is not a lack of technology. It's a lack of shared understanding that surfaces under pressure.

Where trust should grow with capability, it often withers. This part unpacks three real-world scenarios where infrastructure and good intentions weren't enough because alignment was missing from the start.

The ML Misfire

A fintech startup deployed its first fraud model. Infrastructure was ready. Results looked good. But customer complaints soared.

Investigation revealed the failure: training labels were inconsistent. "Uncertain" in one team meant "false positive" in another. The model learned contradiction. What looked like precision was semantic drift.

Models don't know better. They learn what you teach them.

Regional Misalignment: The EdTech Example

An edtech company tracked "student drop-off" across regions. But each locale defined it differently:

- India: no logins
- Brazil: no submissions
- U.S.: declining quiz scores

Executives couldn't make sense of conflicting trends. Behind the scenes, panic set in. Alignment was an afterthought. Fragility followed.

The Retention Trap

A retail chain calculated "customer retention" four different ways across departments. When the CEO asked for clarity, trust had already eroded. Strategic decisions had been made on shifting definitions.

These stories aren't about failure. They're about the fragility that emerges when we scale without shared meaning.

Part 4: Breaking the Illusion

The promise of the modern data stack is compelling: scalable infrastructure, automated pipelines, powerful visualizations, and machine learning at our fingertips. But the illusion begins when these capabilities are mistaken for maturity.

The truth is more sobering: technology amplifies what's already there. Without clarity, trust, and shared meaning, it merely accelerates the spread of confusion. If your foundation is fractured, more pipelines only move noise faster. More dashboards only multiply disagreement.

So, what breaks the illusion?

It's not more technology. It's intentional design. It's starting with language, not logic; with ownership, not outputs; with questions, not tools. Maturity begins not in your cloud bill but in your conversations. The most advanced organizations today don't just move fast, they move coherently. They ensure that what flows through their systems is as aligned as the systems themselves. They invest in culture, contracts, and clarity before scale.

Theme	**Illusion** (signal)	**Reality** (what matters)
Progress	More pipelines	Alignment before automation
Insight	Dashboards	Semantics as the foundation of trust
Transformation	Tool adoption	Design ownership, clarity, intent
Maturity	Activity	Shared understanding and outcomes
Meaning	Metrics	Stewardship and governance
Value (AI)	LLM usage / AI agents shipped	Trusted outcomes with feedback loops

The Path Forward

The only way out of the illusion is through semantic clarity. Here's a pragmatic approach:

1. **Start with Semantics** – Define core terms before building anything.

2. **Assign Ownership** – Every dataset should have a steward.
3. **Treat Data as a Product** – Serve users, track quality, evolve based on feedback.
4. **Measure Trust, Not Volume** – Track adoption, disputes, and satisfaction, not just rows processed.
5. **Align Tech with Outcomes** – Choose tools that reinforce governance and understanding.

Final Reflection: The Mirror, Not the Trophy

Data is not a neutral observer. It's a mirror. It reflects the systems, decisions, and collaborations that create it. If your dashboards conflict or your KPIs confuse, don't blame the tooling.

Ask: what does this reveal about how we think, work, and communicate?

The first step to maturity isn't more tooling. It's introspection.

Are we rewarding motion or meaning? Are we building for clarity or show? Do we treat data as a strategic asset, or an afterthought?

Until we treat data as a mirror, not a crutch, the illusion of progress will persist. And insight will remain just out of reach.

CHAPTER 2

The Software Illusion: Why We Misunderstand Data

"We think we are describing the world we see, but in fact, we are describing the world we think."
— David Eagleman

Introduction: The Origins of Misunderstanding

In a boardroom review, two executives argue over the 'active provider' metric, each pointing to a different dashboard, each citing a different source. Both are right. And both are wrong. Welcome to the world of data.

Despite underpinning digital transformation, data remains one of the most misunderstood assets in modern organizations. The issue isn't a lack of effort, talent, or even investment. It's the silent inheritance of the wrong mental models. This chapter is about the dangers of applying software engineering assumptions to the fundamentally interpretive world of data.

If code is a blueprint, data is the weather report; observed, contextual, and subject to interpretation.

In most organizations, the prevailing approach to data is shaped by software engineering paradigms. We've imported familiar heuristics—modular code, object reuse, API abstractions—and assumed they apply neatly to the world of data. The result? We build data systems with the confidence of software systems, expecting clarity and consistency but data doesn't behave that way.

But data is not software. Unlike code, data is observed, not written. It flows through systems as a consequence of behavior, not instruction. It evolves passively, silently, and often without documentation. The application of software-centric paradigms to data architecture doesn't lead to clarity. It leads to complexity, fragmentation, and data debt.

Consider this common scenario: a team builds a set of microservices for a provider-facing platform. Each service maintains its own database and publishes events to a central pipeline. The engineering is sound, the interfaces are clean, and everything is tested.

Now the analytics team asks: How many active providers did we have last quarter? Simple question. Impossible answer.

Why? Because:

- One team defines a provider as anyone who created an account.
- Another requires a completed purchase.
- A third filters out churned users after 30 days.
- None of this logic lives in a shared place. It's scattered across services, dashboards, and undocumented SQL.

Despite the robust engineering, the organization has no shared understanding of what a "provider" is. The code is clean. The data is a mess.

Reframing the Problem: Tools vs. Truth

To correct this course, we must challenge long-held assumptions. We must treat data problems as questions of meaning, not mechanics; questions about what we know, how we know it, and how reliably we can share that knowledge across teams. That means broadening our perspective on data not as a byproduct of systems, but as a discipline in its own right. It also means restructuring teams, incentives, and processes around a simple but powerful principle: truth over tools.

Only then can we move beyond heroics, eliminate ambiguity, and build systems that empower decision-making with confidence and clarity.

When Good Engineering Goes Bad for Data

Many data issues originate not from poor engineering but from applying software principles to data without accounting for meaning.

Software paradigms like DRY (Don't Repeat Yourself), abstraction, and microservices work because code is authored and controlled.
But data is observed, shared, and interpreted.

- DRY centralizes logic in software, but in data it often leads to over-normalized tables that require fragile joins.
- Object abstraction makes sense in code, but becomes ambiguity when nested structures are flattened for analytics.
- Microservices decentralize ownership, but also fracture core definitions like *provider*, *order*, or *churn*.
- Agile change cycles move fast, but semantic drift moves faster and usually silently.

Imagine a data platform team that builds a "Customer 360" model across multiple sprints. To close stories faster, each squad adjusts column names, joins, or filters to match their own service. By the fourth sprint, "Customer ID" exists in five forms: all valid locally, all divergent globally. Agile success; semantic debt.

In software, failures are visible. In data, failures are silent.

A system can remain technically "correct" while the meaning shifts underneath it, eroding trust long before anyone notices.

Clashing Worldviews: Software vs. Data Thinking

Software engineering and data work operate on fundamentally different assumptions. Software is designed, deterministic, and governed by explicit contracts. Data, by contrast, is observational, shared, and shaped by the real-world behaviors it records. When organizations treat data as if it behaves like software, they unintentionally create ambiguity, drift, and fragmentation.

In software systems, changes are intentional and controlled; failures are visible and immediate. In data systems, change is often silent and emergent; definitions evolve, schemas diverge, and meanings shift without clear ownership. The result is not broken pipelines, but broken understanding. What appears technically functional can be semantically incorrect, leading teams to make decisions based on conflicting or misaligned interpretations of the same data.

Software vs. Data: The Real Friction

Dimension	**Software Mindset**	**Data Reality**
Nature of Output	Authored, deterministic	Observed, contextual, evolving
Change Behavior	Explicit, versioned	Often implicit, untracked
Failure Mode	Fast, visible errors	Slow, silent misinterpretations
Contracts	Enforced by code	Rare, inconsistent, or undocumented
Ownership	Clear team boundaries	Shared, distributed, often ambiguous
Testing	Automated & proactive	Manual, reactive, or absent

Software teams assume stability and explicitness: if the code compiles and tests pass, behavior is reliable. But data reliability depends on shared meaning, lineage, and context; factors rarely captured in code or schema alone. Without a shared semantic foundation, even well-engineered systems produce data that is technically correct yet practically unusable.

The path forward is not more tools, but greater alignment on meaning, a theme developed in later chapters: context, stewardship, and intentional data design.

Illustration: Mismatched Expectations

One of the most persistent sources of dysfunction in modern data work lies in the misalignment of mental models between software engineers and data professionals. Though both groups are technically skilled, they operate with fundamentally different assumptions that quietly collide when data pipelines meet production systems.

✦ Software Developers Expect Stability and Contracts

In software engineering, immutability and enforceable contracts are core design principles. Developers write APIs expecting that:

- Interfaces are stable. If you call a function with the correct parameters, it will behave as expected today and tomorrow.
- Contracts are explicit. Data types are defined. Exceptions are handled. Any breaking change is caught during compile-time or through a robust CI/CD pipeline.
- Quality gates are automated. Unit tests, integration tests, mocks, and static analysis tools provide constant feedback to ensure changes don't break downstream systems.

These expectations are not merely preferences. They're reinforced by tooling and culture. A deployment that fails a test won't ship. A breaking change to a service contract halts the release process.

✦ Data Teams Expect Drift and Chaos

By contrast, data teams live in a world of implicit assumptions, partial information, and silent failures:

- Schemas evolve without notice. A field disappears. A data type silently changes. A new value appears in a categorical column breaking logic that relied on a fixed set.

- No real contract exists. Tables and event streams rarely come with guarantees. They are often shared as-is, discovered via reverse-engineering, and queried by guesswork.
- Testing is ad hoc or reactive. Data quality issues are caught after stakeholders complain about "weird numbers" in a report, not during a formalized pre-deployment phase.

These shifts represent quiet divergences in meaning rather than overt failures in structure. Unlike software, which is written and controlled by a team, data emerges from user behavior, operational systems, and messy business logic.

✦ Tooling Widens the Gap

The divide is not just conceptual; it's amplified by the surrounding ecosystem:

- Software teams use mature CI/CD platforms with automated testing, linting, and enforcement of code-level contracts.
- Data teams, if they have CI at all, often manage schema changes manually and lack automated validation mechanisms.

Few organizations have invested in contract-first data pipelines that:

- Validate schema compatibility across versions
- Enforce column-level constraints
- Track data lineage and blast radius for changes

As a result, data pipelines are often brittle, reactive, and deeply dependent on institutional memory and heroism to stay operational.

Toward a Shared Mental Model

Solving this mismatch requires more than tooling. It requires cultural convergence. Engineers must understand that data is inherently volatile and observational. Data teams must adopt practices that bring rigor to evolution and change. Both must agree on a new shared model:

Data interfaces are real interfaces and they deserve contracts, testing, and observability just like APIs do.

Until this becomes the norm, mismatched expectations will continue to create friction, erode trust, and limit the reliability of data in production systems.

Real-World Friction

Misalignment between software and data expectations is not theoretical, it shows up in everyday operational failures. Small schema changes, repurposed fields, or local interpretations of a value can create organization-wide confusion long before anyone realizes something is wrong.

At a large logistics firm, a software team changed shipment_status from a numeric code to a text label to improve readability in the application UI. The change required no schema migration and passed all application tests. However, a downstream data pipeline used those numeric codes to classify delivery reliability. When the values shifted, the reliability metric flattened unexpectedly. No alerts were triggered because the pipeline still ran successfully. The data was valid but its meaning had changed.

It took three weeks and an executive review meeting to locate the cause. The issue was not tooling. It was assumption drift. The fix did not require new platforms, new dashboards, or new data pipelines. It required: Shared documentation of field definitions, a review process for meaning-affecting changes and a clear owner for each business-critical data element.

When the organization aligned meaning before movement, reliability reporting stabilized, and decision-making regained confidence.

Technical correctness does not guarantee analytical truth.
Without shared semantics, correctness and usefulness diverge.

Bridging the Gap

Bridging the divide between software and data teams requires a shared understanding of how data is used, interpreted, and depended upon across the organization. Software teams must recognize that data is not simply a byproduct of application logic. It is reused, reinterpreted, and extended across domains. Data teams, in turn, must adopt practices that bring rigor and traceability to change.

The shift begins with a simple premise:

Data interfaces are real interfaces. They need contracts, ownership, and review, just like APIs.

Practical enablers include:

- Shared ownership of core definitions across domains
- Change review processes for meaning-affecting schema updates
- Metadata that documents not just structure, but intent and context

As teams adopt a shared mental model, reliability improves not because pipelines are more complex, but because meaning is maintained across the system

Why We Don't Train Engineers to Think in Semantics

The root of most data misunderstanding is educational, not technical. Software engineers are trained to think in terms of logic, efficiency, and systems behavior not in terms of meaning. They learn how to write code that runs, not how to design data that endures interpretation across teams.

Most curricula teach:

- How to normalize tables, but not how to model business concepts?
- How to query data, but not how to maintain semantic consistency over time?
- How to build systems, but not how to ensure different groups interpret data the same way?

The result is predictable: engineers become experts in processing data, but not in explaining it. Business logic becomes buried in pipelines, dashboards, and code that was never intended to define truth.

We teach people how to move data, not how to preserve meaning. This gap does not reflect a lack of intelligence or effort. It reflects a missing discipline.

Until organizations intentionally teach semantic design, data will continue to be technically correct, operationally functional, and strategically misinterpreted.

Data's Real Nature: History, Sharing, and Interpretation

Data is more than input and output. It's the context in which decisions are made, strategies are formed, and progress is measured. When software developers build systems, they focus on instructions, flows, and outcomes. Data, on the other hand, is less about execution and more about representation. It encodes real-world states: a completed transaction, a failed login, an abandoned cart.

Yet we often manage data like code; static, logical, and self-contained. That's a mistake. Unlike code, data is historical, social, and interpretive. Code either works or fails. A data row may be wrong, transformed from elsewhere, or misread downstream.

To truly understand data, we must elevate our thinking. We must view it not as a byproduct of applications, but as an evolving narrative that must be preserved, explained, and stewarded.

Core Differences Between Code and Data

1. **Data Has History**: Every data point has a lineage. A single value might have originated in a web form, passed through validation logic, transformed in a pipeline, and landed in a warehouse and losing or gaining meaning along the way.
2. **Data Is Shared**: Unlike code, which may run in isolation, data is reused across departments, tools, and processes. Any change has ripple effects.
3. **Data Demands Interpretation**: A "churned" provider in marketing may be considered "at-risk" in finance or "inactive" in operations. These interpretations must be aligned and documented.

Case Study: Misunderstood Metrics in Retail

A multinational retail chain launched a loyalty rewards program and began measuring "active providers." Marketing defined activity as one transaction in the last 90 days. Finance used the average balance of loyalty points. Product teams used app login frequency.

Each team published metrics using their logic. Executives received three different figures during a quarterly strategy meeting causing delays, blame, and credibility issues. To move from metric confusion to governed quality, Chapter 10 introduces frameworks that define and operationalize trust, ownership, and clarity across the data landscape.

A task force unified definitions and documented them in a semantic layer tied to dashboard filters and data catalog tags. In the following quarter, cross-functional alignment improved dramatically, and meetings focused on action, not clarification.

Modern data architecture must be built around meaning. That means:

- Schemas must represent shared understanding, not just source layouts.
- Data models must reflect business intent.
- Definitions must be versioned and explainable.

Metadata becomes critical. Without context, a field labeled event_flag is just noise. With metadata, we understand it means "user completed onboarding" and is based on a sequence of three prior actions. Now it's valuable.

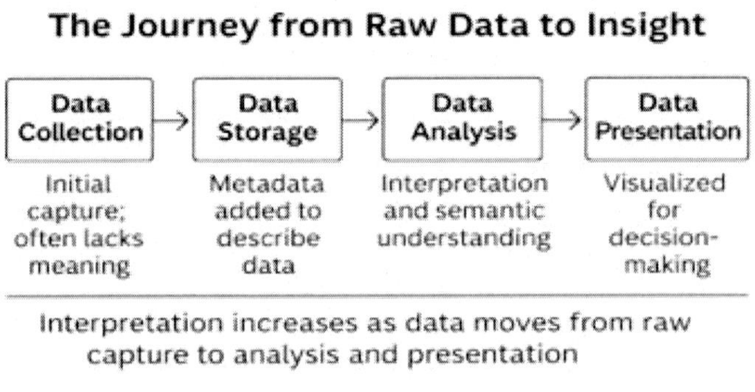

Figure 2.1 The journey from raw data to insight, as interpretation increases from collection to presentation.

Bringing Context to Life: Practical Steps

- Integrate business glossary tools directly into BI tools and query environments.
- Include descriptions, source info, and usage notes in every dataset published.
- Create feedback loops where data consumers flag confusing fields or broken assumptions.

When we design data systems that preserve context, we reduce errors, accelerate insight, and build trust. In a world where analytics informs everything from hiring to policy to pricing, losing context isn't just inefficient. It's dangerous. To avoid this, organizations must shift from seeing data as a code artifact to treating it as a living narrative. That shift unlocks the true value of data.

Designing Data Like You Mean It

Most organizations still treat data as a byproduct of systems rather than a product with users, expectations, and quality requirements. When data is treated as exhaust from applications, no one owns its meaning, purpose, or long-term usability. The result is familiar: duplicated logic, inconsistent metrics, and recurring clarification work.

A data product mindset changes this. A data product is not just a table or a pipeline; it is a shared, trustworthy representation of a business concept that others rely on. It has a purpose, consumers, and a clear definition of what "good" means.

The shift is simple: Pipelines move data. Products create understanding.

A well-designed data product has:

- **Clear ownership** — a steward accountable for quality and interpretation
- **Defined meaning** — what each field represents and how it should be used
- **Versioned logic** — changes are explicit, reviewed, and discoverable
- **A known audience** — built for real decision-making and reuse

Example: Instead of multiple teams recalculating "active provider" in different ways, a curated provider_activity data product defines:

- What "active" means
- How it is calculated
- How often it is updated
- Who to contact when something needs review

This eliminates metric drift, reduces rework, and minimizes dependence on tribal knowledge. When data is designed and stewarded like a product, trust increases not because more dashboards are created, but because meaning is shared and stable.

Governance as a Driver of Clarity

Data governance is often misunderstood as control, restriction, or bureaucracy. In reality, effective governance is what enables data to be trusted, reused, and interpreted consistently across teams. It is not about slowing delivery. It is about ensuring that the data being delivered actually means the same thing to everyone who uses it.

A business glossary is central to this shift. It defines core concepts—such as "provider," "churn," or "active account"—in clear, unambiguous language. These definitions serve as shared reference points across analytics, operations, and product teams. When language is shared, decisions align. When definitions drift, trust erodes.

However, a glossary only works when it is *owned and maintained.* That requires clear roles:

- **Data Stewards** ensure the accuracy and consistency of key definitions.
- **Domain Leads** resolve conflicts when terms overlap across business areas.
- **Governance Councils** approve changes and ensure definitions reflect organizational priorities.

Metadata platforms help operationalize this work by linking definitions directly to datasets, models, dashboards, and code. When users can trace a metric to its source, see who owns it, and understand how it is calculated, trust increases and reliance on informal interpretation decreases.

Governance, when done well, does not constrain teams. It accelerates them. It allows data to be reused confidently, interpreted consistently, and communicated clearly. It reduces rework, clarifies accountability, and provides the foundation for meaningful, scalable analytics. Governance is not a gate. It is the architecture of shared meaning.

If misunderstanding data is the root, the next challenge is ownership; who defines, governs, and sustains meaning across the enterprise.

CHAPTER 3

Data Strategy and Ownership in Large Organizations

"Strategy without execution is hallucination."
— Thomas Edison

The Mirage of Ownership in Interoperability

A national health insurer deployed a centralized analytics platform to unify claims, eligibility, and provider data. All systems were technically compliant with FHIR guidelines and HIPAA regulatory standards. Yet regional care quality dashboards still reported different readmission rates. One division counted only inpatient discharges; another included outpatient visits. Both numbers were defensible. Neither was shared.

The interoperability was real at the *data format* level but not at the *semantic* level. The failure wasn't in the stack. It was in ownership. No one was responsible for defining what "readmission" meant across contexts, and each unit assumed its own definition was correct.

Compliance creates standardization of exchange. Ownership creates standardization of meaning. Infrastructure scaled the data. But only ownership could have aligned the understanding.

Infrastructure scaled the data. But only ownership could have aligned the understanding.

Nominal Ownership vs. Actual Stewardship

Aspect	Nominal Ownership	Actual Stewardship
Definition	A title assigned in governance documentation	A responsibility exercised in daily data decisions
Focus	Compliance and sign-off	Quality, usability, and continuous improvement
Authority	Symbolic—little power over systems or data models	Active—can influence schemas, processes, and access
Behavior	Defends scope, avoids accountability	Collaborates, resolves conflicts, enables reuse
Visibility	Present in org charts	Evident in how data issues are addressed
Outcome	Ownership in name only	Stewardship in practice and culture

True governance doesn't depend on who signs the policy document, but on who protects the data's meaning when no one is watching.

Why Strategy Fails Without Ownership

In large organizations, data strategy fails not because the technology is insufficient, but because ownership is unclear. Modern platforms can centralize storage and standardize access, but they cannot resolve disagreements about meaning. When no one owns core definitions or is accountable for their evolution, each team applies its own interpretation, and the organization produces multiple "truths." Dashboards conflict, reports are debated, and leadership loses confidence; not in the tools, but in the data itself.

You can modernize the stack. But without ownership of meaning, strategy cannot execute. What follows is a practical breakdown of the core areas where strategy fails without ownership, and the patterns that enable alignment to be rebuilt.

Section 1: Bridging the IT-Business Divide

The divide between IT departments and business units is structural, not merely communicative. Typically, IT manages centralized data infrastructure, while decentralized business units expect insightful outputs. This disconnects results in unassigned responsibilities for data quality, misaligned KPIs, and fragile dashboards that fail with schema alterations.

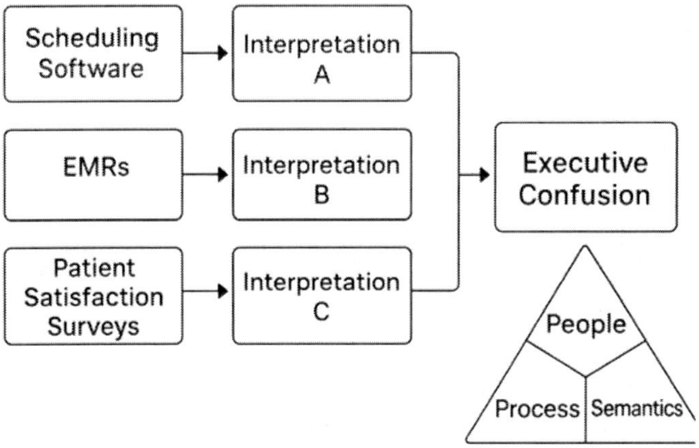

Figure 3.1 Conflicting interpretations from multiple systems leading to executive confusion across people, process, and semantics.

Example: The Reporting Crisis

Consider a large healthcare provider that faced discrepancies in patient wait-time reporting. Three departments independently generated wait-time reports from different sources (scheduling software, electronic medical records (EMRs), and patient satisfaction surveys etc.) yielding conflicting data presented to executives. When logic lives inside Looker dashboards or Power BI reports without peer review or documentation, truth becomes a matter of tooling, not governance.

The fundamental issue wasn't technical incompetence but lack of ownership over "wait time" semantics. IT handled technical pipelines but did not manage semantic clarity. Analysts independently interpreted definitions, causing confusion and mistrust.

Typical indicators of IT-business misalignment include:

- Duplicate reports presenting inconsistent figures.
- Dashboards built but seldom trusted.
- Business logic buried within ETL scripts, inaccessible and unclear.

Alignment requires establishing shared language, defined roles, and strategies that connect technology directly to business outcomes.

What Business Sees vs. What IT Sees

Aspect	Business Users See	IT / Data Teams See
Dashboard	A clean, interactive report with key metrics	A fragile chain of joins, filters, and calculated fields
"Customer Count"	A single number displayed on screen	Five conflicting queries from inconsistent source systems

Metric Labels	Clear terms like "Active Customers" or "Revenue Growth"	Undefined terms lacking glossary mapping or owner
System Downtime	"Why is the dashboard broken again?"	A schema change upstream caused pipeline failure
Feature Request	"Can we just add a column for status?"	Requires data model changes, ETL updates, testing, and validation
Governance	"We don't need red tape we need answers"	No metadata, no lineage, no documentation making reuse and trust impossible
Response Time	"Why does IT take so long to make small changes?"	Change requests are unprioritized, under-documented, and high-risk
Ownership	"Data is just there—why does someone need to own it?"	Ownership is unclear, leading to firefighting instead of proactive resolution

Section 2: Clarity in Complex Ownership

Ambiguous data ownership is one of the most persistent barriers to data maturity in large organizations. When no one is accountable for the meaning, quality, or lifecycle of a dataset, teams make their own assumptions. Over time, this leads to diverging definitions, duplicated reporting logic, and dashboards that cannot be reconciled.

Ownership gaps often appear in federated environments—universities, hospital systems, government agencies, insurers—where multiple business units contribute data but no single team owns its semantics.

The result isn't just confusion; it is operational risk. When definitions can be interpreted differently, metrics can be defended but not trusted.

Example: Municipal Vendor Invoice Dashboard

A city government attempted to centralize vendor payment tracking across procurement, finance, legal, and controller departments. The technical integration succeeded; data pipelines were stable and refreshed automatically. But the dashboards failed.

Each department defined key lifecycle stages differently:

Stage	Procurement Definition	Finance Definition
Invoice Received	Logged in procurement software	Entered into ERP
Invoice Approved	Clerk approval	Budget officer approval
Invoice Paid	Remittance initiated	Funds cleared

From a data perspective, the same invoice could appear "received," "approved," or "paid" depending on the department.

Executives saw lagging compliance metrics and contradictory cycle-time reports. Trust collapsed not because of data quality issues, but because ownership of meaning was never assigned.

The breakthrough came only when:

1. A data steward was named for the vendor invoice domain.
2. Each stage was documented with clear business definitions.

3. Dashboards were linked to a shared glossary, not team-specific logic.

Once semantic ownership was established, reconciliation time decreased, dashboards aligned, and decision-making accelerated.

Symptoms of Ownership Ambiguity vs. Healthy Stewardship

If Ownership Is Unclear	If Stewardship Is Defined
Multiple teams generate conflicting metrics	One certified version of key metrics exists
Business logic buried in ETL or SQL	Logic defined in semantic layer or glossary
Analysts ask IT for clarification	Questions go to domain steward / owner
Dashboards are debated, not used	Dashboards are trusted and referenced

What Changes When Ownership Is Explicit

- Definitions stop drifting.
- Data quality issues have a clear escalation path.
- Analysts stop reverse-engineering meaning.
- Executives regain confidence in KPIs.

Ownership is not just a governance artifact. It is the precondition for trust.

Section 3: Crafting an Actionable Data Strategy

A data strategy is not a platform roadmap, a cloud migration plan, or a list of dashboards to build. It is a system for how meaning, ownership, and trust are created and sustained across the organization.

Most strategies fail because they stop at vision. The strategy document sounds aligned, but the execution environment is not. Tools are purchased, architectures drawn, and committees formed but the core questions remain unanswered:

- Who owns this data?
- What does this metric mean, exactly?
- How do changes get communicated and governed?

A real data strategy answers these questions in operational terms.

Example: University Data Governance Transformation

A major public university tried to unify enrollment analytics across admissions, financial aid, and academic advising. Every department calculated "active student" differently:

Department	Definition Used
Admissions	Student with an accepted offer
Registrar	Student enrolled in any course
Financial Aid	Student with disbursed funds
Advising	Student who met with advisor in last 60 days

Technologically, the integration was successful. Semantically, it failed.

The university corrected the issue by establishing:

1. A University Data Council with cross-department representation.
2. A shared glossary defining key student lifecycle states.
3. Named stewards for each domain (Admissions, Registrar, Financial Aid, Advising).
4. A rule: Dashboards must pull from certified definitions.

The impact was immediate: reporting disputes dropped, onboarding accelerated, and executive planning shifted from clarification → decision.

The Three Pillars of Actionable Strategy

Pillar	**Purpose**	**What It Looks Like in Practice**
Ownership	Makes accountability explicit	Every dataset and metric has a named owner
Shared Semantics	Ensures meaning is consistent	Glossary definitions tied to data models and BI
Execution Loops	Keeps alignment alive as systems evolve	Regular review, versioning, issue escalation, feedback channels

A strategy without ownership is philosophy. A strategy without semantics is noise. A strategy without execution loops decays.

A mature data strategy is not a document but a design discipline; one that links ownership with execution, and accountability with meaning. A data strategy succeeds when meaning, ownership, and trust become operational, not conceptual. The goal is not alignment once, it is alignment continuously, embedded into roles, workflows, and decision-making.

Section 4: Designing for Government Reality

Public sector organizations face unique constraints that shape how data strategy must function. Unlike the private sector, where platforms and processes can be changed quickly, government entities operate under regulatory oversight, lengthy procurement cycles, and cross-agency coordination requirements. These constraints make semantic alignment and ownership even more critical, because changes are slow and the costs of confusion are public.

Example: Federal Open Data Portal Reform

A national agency launched a public-facing open data portal to increase transparency. The data was technically available, but lacked

documentation and clear definitions. Journalists and public policy analysts misinterpreted key metrics, leading to criticism and confusion. The issue was not data quality. It was missing semantic context.

The agency corrected the problem by:

1. Adding metadata and field-level explanations.
2. Publishing a semantic usage guide alongside key dataset.
3. Assigning domain stewards responsible for managing updates and answering public inquiries.

Trust improved because the agency clarified meaning, not because it changed its technology.

Constraint	Impact on Data Strategy
Slow procurement cycles	Tools cannot solve alignment gaps quickly; semantics must be correct upfront.
High public scrutiny	Misinterpretation becomes a reputational and political risk.
Multi-agency coordination	Definitions must be shared *across* organizations, not just within one.
Legal compliance and auditability	Lineage and explainability are not optional, they are mandatory.

In government, ambiguity is costly, and clarity is a governance requirement.

What Works in Government Contexts

To be effective, public sector data strategies must:

- Document meaning upfront (glossaries, semantic layers, usage notes).
- Assign accountable ownership, even when agencies share responsibility.
- Version definitions, not just schemas.
- Design for explainability and audit trails, not just delivery.

This is not extra bureaucracy. This is what prevents public confusion, audit failure, and system rework. Public sector data strategy cannot rely on speed or tool flexibility. It must rely on semantic precision, transparent ownership, and explicit documentation.

Section 5: Federated Models with Central Coordination

Large organizations often fall into one of two extremes:

- Centralized control, where a single enterprise team attempts to govern everything. This stalls adoption, slows delivery, and breeds workarounds.
- Fully decentralized autonomy, where business units move fast but definitions diverge, dashboards conflict, and trust erodes.

Neither model works at scale. The most effective approach is federated governance: Domains own their data products, while shared semantics and standards are centrally coordinated. This model preserves relevance and agility without sacrificing alignment.

Example: Insurance Consortium Data Exchange

A multi-state insurance consortium needed comparable reporting across different regulatory environments. Each state retained its own systems and local processes. But all states agreed to:

- A shared glossary for key entities (claim, enrollee, adjudication)
- Standardized data contracts for exchange
- Central certification of published metrics

Each domain (state) controlled its local pipelines, but meaning was centrally governed.

The result:

- Local autonomy remained intact.
- Cross-state analytics became trustworthy.

- Reporting disputes declined.
- Audits passed cleanly.

This is the value of federation done correctly:
Local control + shared meaning = scalable trust.

The Four Layers of Effective Federated Governance

Layer	**Purpose**	**Owner**
1. **Domain Ownership**	Each domain manages its own data product logic and quality.	Domain Data Product Owners
2. **Shared Semantic Layer (Glossary + Contracts)**	Ensures consistent definitions across domains.	Central Data Governance Council
3. **Shared Platform & Metadata Services**	Provides lineage, cataloging, access control, and observability.	Enterprise Data Platform Team
4. **Contract Enforcement & Certification**	Tests, validates, and approves domain outputs before sharing.	Data Quality & Trust Office

This structure allows:

- Autonomy where knowledge is deep (domains)
- Consistency where alignment is essential (enterprise)

Why Federation Works

- Meaning stays consistent, even when systems differ.
- Ownership is clear, reducing reliance on "data heroes."
- Changes scale, because semantic clarity is versioned and coordinated.

Federation is not about splitting responsibility. It is about assigning it precisely. Federated governance succeeds only when: Ownership lives in domains, and Meaning is standardized centrally. This is how large organizations achieve speed without fragmentation and trust without bottlenecks.

Section 6: Measuring and Sustaining Trust

Trust is the real currency of data. If data is not trusted, it is not used; no matter how modern the platform or how elegant the dashboards.

Yet most organizations never measure trust. They track data volume, model accuracy, and pipeline throughput, but not whether decision-makers believe the data enough to act on it. To sustain data maturity over time, trust must become a visible, trackable performance indicator, not an assumption.

Example: The Data Trust Index in Financial Services

A financial services organization introduced a Data Trust Index to evaluate its most critical datasets. Each dataset was scored on:

Dimension	Description
Lineage Transparency	Can users trace where the data came from?
Data Quality Signals	Are errors monitored and surfaced automatically?

Semantic Clarity	Is the meaning unambiguous and documented?
Owner Responsiveness	Are issues resolved quickly and consistently?

Datasets with high trust scores were marked certified and prioritized for enterprise dashboards and analytical modeling. Low-scoring datasets were flagged for stewardship and remediation.

Trust became visible, not assumed.

Executives stopped asking which numbers were correct. They knew which datasets were authoritative.

How to Measure Trust (Simple, Adoptable Framework)

Score each critical dataset **1–5** across four dimensions:

Dataset	Lineage	Quality	Clarity	Ownership	Trust Score
Customer Master	5	4	5	4	**18** (High)
Patient Intake Logs	3	2	2	1	**8** (Low)
Invoice History	4	5	3	4	**16** (High)
Marketing Leads	2	3	2	3	**10** (Medium)

Interpretation:

- **High score** → safe for enterprise dashboards and ML use
- **Medium score** → suitable with caution; needs review

- **Low score** → must be remediated before reuse

This turns trust from opinion → governance signal → investment priority.

How Trust Is Sustained

Trust is not a project. Trust is a behavior system reinforced over time.

To sustain trust:

1. Certify core data products and label them in BI tools.
2. Track adoption as a proxy for perceived value.
3. Reward stewards in performance evaluations, not just engineers.
4. Review key semantics quarterly, not annually.
5. Make trust dashboards visible to producers and consumers alike.

The goal is not to enforce control. The goal is to enable confident decision-making at scale.

Data maturity is not defined by tooling or scale, but by trust that data reflects shared meaning. Measuring trust operationalizes alignment—and preserves it as organizations grow.

The Cost of Misaligned Strategies

Most failed data strategies don't collapse due to a lack of ambition but from a lack of alignment. Across industries, even well-funded and technically advanced initiatives unravel because critical teams operate with mismatched definitions, timelines, and goals.

Case 1: Risk Without a Shared Foundation

At a global bank, an advanced ML-based credit risk model was developed to automate loan approvals. Technically, the model performed well in staging. But in production, branches across regions fed in data from different "trusted" sources. The risk team used historical default data from the warehouse, while the sales team prioritized a CRM-integrated scoring system. Meanwhile, operations flagged discrepancies in address formats and income verification. What resulted wasn't just confusion. It was regulatory risk.

Despite massive investment, the bank had no unified semantic layer to define customer identity or creditworthiness. The data strategy was a patchwork of tool integrations, not a cohesive foundation. Alignment was assumed. Failure followed.

Case 2: Unified Portal, Fragmented Patients

A large healthcare system deployed a new "unified patient experience" platform, aiming to consolidate EHR, lab results, and billing into a single interface. However, the EHR identified patients based on medical record numbers; billing used insurance account IDs; and lab systems tagged entries by external lab identifiers. When the platform launched, many patients appeared twice. Some lab results didn't match. Legal and compliance teams were alarmed. Confidence in the system plummeted.

The issue wasn't technical; it was a semantic misalignment across systems. The underlying data architecture treated "patient" differently across domains, yet leadership had never reconciled these definitions. They had a platform, but no shared meaning.

The Deeper Pattern

In both examples, the cost wasn't just financial. It was operational risk, reputational damage, and user distrust. These misfires stemmed from a belief that strategy could be implicit. That alignment would emerge organically from execution. That tools could make up for organizational silence.

But in reality, misaligned data strategies are the hidden tax on progress. They slow delivery, amplify confusion, and erode trust faster than any tool can rebuild it. A good data strategy is less about ambition and more about translation: turning business priorities into shared meaning, and shared meaning into trustworthy systems.

CHAPTER 4

The Illusion of Clarity - What is Data, Really?

"The real problem is not whether machines think but whether men do."
— B.F. Skinner

The Illusion of Clarity

Dashboards often create the impression of shared understanding. Numbers look precise. Charts appear authoritative. But clarity at the interface does not guarantee clarity in meaning.

Consider a leadership review where two revenue reports, sourced from the same warehouse, show different totals. One includes cancellations; the other applies currency conversion differently. Both reflect valid logic. Neither reflects shared meaning.

The breakdown is not technical. It's semantic.

We mistake clean tables and polished visuals for alignment. But unless teams agree on definitions, scope, and interpretation, data becomes a Rorschach test, each person sees what they expect.

Clarity is not a product of pipelines. It is a product of language. And language is negotiated, not automated.

This chapter clarifies what data *is* and *is not*. It introduces the idea that meaning - not volume, technology, or model sophistication - is the real bottleneck in data maturity.

1. Semantic Ladder: From Data to Wisdom

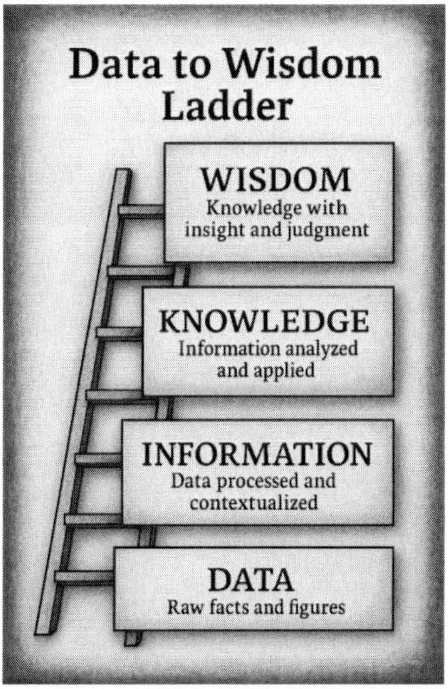

Figure 4.1 The data-to-wisdom ladder (DIKW model)

Organizations often use "data-driven" to imply precision. But *data* is only the lowest rung in a ladder that leads to decision-making.

Layer	What It Represents	Failure Mode When Misunderstood
Data	Raw observations	Appears neutral but lacks context
Information	Organized and contextualized data	Meaning assumed, not verified
Knowledge	Patterns interpreted through domain understanding	Conflicting interpretations
Wisdom	Judged actions under uncertainty	Decisions made on shaky ground

Let's walk through each level with clarity:

Data
At the base, data is a recorded observation, a value without inherent meaning. A timestamp. A boolean. A string. Data can be collected, stored, and moved in immense volumes, but on its own it is inert. Data tells us *that something happened*, not *why it happened* or *what it implies*.
For example, the value **5.6** is meaningless until we know its unit (minutes, dollars, miles), context (average session length, order quantity), and source system (mobile analytics, IoT device, survey response).

Information
Information emerges when data is organized and given context. Metadata, labeling, and categorization begin to shape raw values into interpretable signals.
If we know that **5.6** refers to the *average session length (in minutes)* for *new mobile users* in *Q2*, we have transformed data into information.

But here, semantics become critical: *What exactly counts as a "session"?* Without shared definition, the transformation remains technically correct but semantically fragile.

Knowledge

Knowledge develops when information is interpreted with domain understanding. It reflects comparisons, patterns, cause-and-effect reasoning, and accumulated experience.

Knowledge requires tacit understanding; business logic, institutional memory, and shared conceptual grounding.

If different teams use the same metric with subtly different assumptions, they do not share knowledge. They share *confident disagreement.*

Wisdom

Wisdom is the capacity to make sound decisions under uncertainty. It integrates judgment, ethics, trade-offs, and foresight. In data terms, wisdom is recognizing when *not* to act on a metric because its context is incomplete. It is understanding which KPIs matter in crisis and which can be safely ignored.

Wisdom is not the output of a dashboard. It is the application of human discernment to what the data suggests.

The Invisible Handovers

Each step in this ladder involves a semantic handover — a translation of meaning. These transitions are where misalignment creeps in:

- Data engineers believe they deliver *information*, but may provide only *data.*
- Analysts believe they interpret *knowledge*, but may be operating on inconsistent semantics.
- Executives believe they are making *wise decisions*, but may be reacting to ambiguous numbers presented with confidence.

These gaps manifest not as philosophical errors, but as conflicting dashboards, mis-forecasted trends, and failed AI models.

Designing for the Ladder

Designing trustworthy data systems requires deliberate attention to meaning, not just structure. We must design the transitions imbedding semantics into models, tests, lineage, and contracts.
The goal is not simply to move data efficiently. It is to construct a staircase of meaning where each step is stable, explicit, and shared so that the final destination is not just a number, but *understanding*.

2. Data as a Product

"Data as a product" is often repeated but rarely implemented. Treating data as a product is not about renaming datasets or adding version numbers to dashboards. It is a shift in accountability and intent. It means designing data with users in mind, not as a byproduct of applications, but as something packaged, supported, and continuously improved.

Today, most data pipelines operate like unmanaged supply chains: upstream systems push changes, downstream consumers absorb the consequences, and no one owns the end-to-end experience. Analysts and data scientists are left guessing what fields mean, how reliable a dataset is, or whether a change was intentional. This is how technical assets turn into organizational confusion.

Treating data as a product changes that dynamic. A data product:

- Serves a defined user or decision-making purpose.
- Has a clear owner responsible for quality and clarity.
- Evolves based on feedback and changing business needs.
- Is documented, tested, and versioned—intentionally.

When data is treated as infrastructure, it accumulates debt. When treated as a product, it accumulates trust.

Why This Matters

Most data failures stem from two gaps:

1. Trust – People won't use data they don't understand or believe.
2. Accountability – When issues appear, no one is clearly responsible.

A product mindset reverses both. Producers are accountable for consumer experience, and consumers gain clarity, not guesswork. Governance becomes an attribute of delivery, not a separate committee or late-stage review.

The Roles that operationalize data-as-product:

- Data Product Owner – Defines purpose, scope, and semantic clarity.
- Data Steward – Maintains definitions, lineage, and documentation.
- Data Reliability Engineer – Builds observability and tests into the delivery path.

These do *not* replace engineering roles. They protect them from rework, triage, and semantic firefighting.

Anti-Pattern: Data as an Artifact

When no one owns meaning:

- Tables accumulate without lineage.
- Metrics diverge across teams.

- Dashboards look polished but are not trusted.

These are accidental data products. They appear complete, but they are unfit for confident decision-making.

From Pipelines to Purpose

When data is treated as a product:

- Documentation becomes part of delivery.
- Definitions are embedded in contracts, not tribal memory.
- Versioning is practiced, not avoided.
- Consumers are supported, not blamed.

The simplest test of product thinking is this:

If I had not built this dataset, would I trust it enough to make a decision with it?

If the answer is no, the work is not done.

3. Aligning Semantics: Data as Language

Data is often described as the "new oil" or "digital gold," but a more accurate metaphor is this: data is language. Not just a record of events, but a structured attempt to describe reality. Like language, data is shaped by context, assumptions, and interpretation. It can be precise or ambiguous, shared or disputed. And like language, it only works when meaning is aligned.

This view explains why two teams can analyze the same dataset and reach opposite conclusions. Why integration projects stall even when schemas match. Why dashboards multiply without converging on a single source of truth. The limiting factor is rarely data volume or pipeline performance. The real bottleneck is shared meaning.

Semantics as the Source of Misunderstanding

Most data systems treat structure as truth. If the schema matches and pipelines run, the system is considered correct. But structure is not meaning.

A field named status may represent:

- Payment state (Billing)
- Eligibility state (Enrollment)
- Workflow progress (Operations)

Technically identical. Semantically incompatible.

This is where silent errors are born. Analysts join tables that appear aligned but aren't. Metrics drift across regions. Dashboards contradict each other. The organization isn't suffering from a data problem; it's suffering from a *meaning* problem.

The Hidden Complexity of "Shared" Data

A table named *Customer Profile* may exist across the enterprise, but:

Domain	Who Counts as a "Customer"
Sales	Anyone with an open opportunity
Billing	Anyone with an active invoice
Compliance	Only KYC (Know Your Customer) -verified entities

All correct locally. All conflicting globally.

Without explicit alignment, every analysis becomes translation and every translation introduces risk.

Designing for Semantic Alignment

True alignment requires designing for meaning, not just for storage or transport. Three practices enable this:

1. **Semantic Contracts**
   Define business meaning, not just field names and types.
   What counts as an "active provider"?
   What is the time window for "retention"?
   These definitions must be explicit, shared, and versioned.
2. **Glossaries and Ontologies**
   Begin with a glossary, evolve into relationships.
   "A visit has a diagnosis."
   "A provider may belong to multiple organizations."
   Meaning is structural.
3. **Contextual Metadata**
   Every dataset should state:
   - Where it came from
   - How it is intended to be used
   - Where its interpretation can go wrong

From Technical Joins to Semantic Bridges

When semantics align:

- Reports converge instead of conflict
- Metrics become portable across platforms
- Analysts spend less time interpreting and more time deciding

Semantic alignment is not a one-time cleanup. It is a continuous design practice embedded into modeling, governance, and delivery.

Data Fluency: The New Organizational Literacy

Data fluency is not SQL proficiency. It is the ability to question meaning.

A data-fluent organization regularly asks:

"What does this metric *mean*, specifically?"

"How is this field defined in this context?"

"Who owns this definition, and how is it maintained?"

Fluency is the awareness that a familiar term may not mean what you assume. That awareness is the foundation of trust.

4. What Good Looks Like: A Working Definition

If semantic alignment is the goal, what does success actually look like? In large organizations with many teams, systems, and evolving priorities, "clarity" can feel abstract. But it is observable. Semantic excellence leaves a trail of predictable behavior, fewer surprises, and decisions made with confidence rather than debate.

A practical definition of *good* in this context:

Semantic alignment exists when data consumers can reliably interpret and use data as intended without tribal knowledge, reverse-engineering, or repeated clarification.

This state does not come from perfect tools or exhaustive documentation. It comes from repeatable practices that embed meaning into the data lifecycle from modeling and testing to consumption and versioning.

Markers of Semantic Maturity

Organizations that achieve semantic alignment share common operating patterns:

1. Definitions Are Explicit and Endorsed

- Critical business terms (e.g., *active provider*, *open claim*, *churned user*) are defined collaboratively not inferred from code.
- Definitions are documented, versioned, and tied to real data structures.
- Changes follow a managed review and communication process.

2. Field-Level Meaning Is Captured at Design Time

- Fields carry contextual metadata (units, business rules, lifecycle state), not just names and types.
- Producers are responsible for communicating meaning, not only structure.

3. Consumers Know What They Are Using

- Data products include usage guidance and caveats.
- Metrics are consistent across warehouses, dashboards, and contracts.
- No one has to "ask around" to verify how a metric is defined.

4. Contracts Validate Meaning, Not Just Format

- Data contracts enforce allowable values and business logic, not just schemas.
- Semantic rules are continuously tested not only at deployment events.

5. Feedback Loops Are Embedded

- Consumers have a clear path to raise semantic questions or corrections.
- Producers are incentivized to improve clarity, not just ship data.
- Governance is collaborative, not policing.

What "Good" Feels Like

- Analysts do not chase teams for explanation; the meaning is already present.
- Product owners trust telemetry because definitions were aligned at design.
- Engineers modifying a pipeline know exactly what the semantic impact will be.

This reduces cognitive overhead, accelerates delivery, and builds durable trust.

Not trust in the system's *appearance* but trust in its *meaning*.

What Good Is Not

Semantic alignment does not mean:

- Every term must be modeled in an ontology.
- Ambiguity is eliminated forever.
- Debate disappears.

Instead: Ambiguity is surfaced early, resolved intentionally, and documented transparently. Meaning becomes a designed property, not tribal memory.

A Living Standard, not a Static Ideal

Semantic clarity must evolve. Business meaning changes. Regulations shift. Markets introduce new patterns. "Good" today may drift tomorrow. So, the goal is not semantic *perfection*, it is semantic resilience.

Resilience comes from embedding semantics into:

- Roles (owners, stewards)
- Processes (versioning, communication loops)
- Platforms (metadata, contracts, semantic tests)

When meaning is treated as a first-class concern, data becomes not just available but usable, trusted, and transformative.

5. Semantic Drift: How Trust Erodes

Semantic drift is the silent killer of long-term data trust. Organizations often focus on pipeline reliability, schema enforcement, and dashboard polish. Meanwhile, the real risk grows quietly: the gradual loss of shared meaning.

Semantic drift occurs when the intended meaning of a field, metric, or entity changes over time, usually without being formally acknowledged. The data still *looks* correct. The pipelines still *run. But what the* data *means* has shifted.

The result: metrics that used to align begin diverging. Dashboards disagree. Teams debate numbers instead of discussing decisions.
What was once clarity becomes confusion.

This is how semantic debt forms not in dramatic failure, but in silent, incremental erosion.

How Drift Happens

Semantic drift rarely announces itself. It creeps in through common organizational realities:

- A feature update changes how an "active user" is counted, but dashboards don't update.
- A team reorganizes and institutional knowledge disappears with departures.
- A field originally meant for one purpose gets repurposed for multiple, conflicting workflows.
- Regional variations evolve without review or communication.
- System migrations change structure without revisiting meaning.

Example: In a global healthcare firm, encounter_type originally captured *outpatient* vs *inpatient.* Over time, telehealth, home visits, and messaging encounters were added under the same field without redefining the concept. Reports became inconsistent. Analysts blamed data quality.
The real problem: the meaning had changed while the label had not.

The Cost of Semantic Debt

Like technical debt, semantic debt compounds:

- More time spent reconciling dashboards across teams.
- Multiple versions of the same metric circulate, all "correct."
- Onboarding becomes reliant on tribal knowledge.
- Models degrade, not because of data quality, but because the *data no longer means what the model assumes.*

Worst of all, trust erodes even when the data is structurally sound. If people don't trust the meaning, they won't trust the output.

Detecting Drift Early

Early warning signs include:

- Frequent questions like *"What does this field actually represent?"*
- Parallel dashboards built to "double-check the numbers."
- Catalog definitions that don't match real operational usage.
- Model performance drops while pipelines remain stable.

If you're seeing these, drift has already begun.

Strategies to Contain and Correct Drift

1. Semantic Versioning

Treat changes in meaning like API changes. When a definition evolves, *version it*, document it, communicate it.

2. Metadata-Aware Monitoring

Track not just schema changes, but semantic lineage; how definitions propagate across models, dashboards, and features.

3. Stewardship with Shared Ownership

Designate term stewards for key business concepts. Stewards own meaning, not just structure.

4. Add Meaning, Don't Overload Fields

If a term takes on new interpretations, introduce a new field. Preserve the original semantics. Do not mutate them silently.

5. Semantic Assertions in Pipelines

Data quality checks cannot stop at type validation. They must also verify that values make sense within the business context they represent.

Contracts must include *meaning constraints* (e.g., allowed value states).

Syntactic vs. Semantic Validity

Aspect	Syntactic Validity	Semantic Validity
Definition	Structure is correct	Meaning is correct
Example Pass	2024-01-10 is valid date	Revenue is not negative for a completed transaction
Detects	Missing fields, wrong types	Misinterpretation, logic drift, outdated assumptions
Risk if Ignored	Pipeline fails	Decisions mislead, trust collapses
Enforced by	Parsers, validators	Business rules, stewards, governance

Paying Down Semantic Debt

Semantic debt cannot be eliminated.
But it can be recognized, tracked, and managed by making meaning:

- **Visible** (linked to data models and dashboards)
- **Versioned** (changes recorded, communicated)
- **Tested** (assertions embedded in pipelines)

- **Reviewed continuously**, not annually

This shifts semantics from *implicit understanding* → explicit organizational asset.

Meaning will drift unless it is intentionally designed, maintained, and communicated. Trust is not preserved by accident. it is preserved by stewardship.

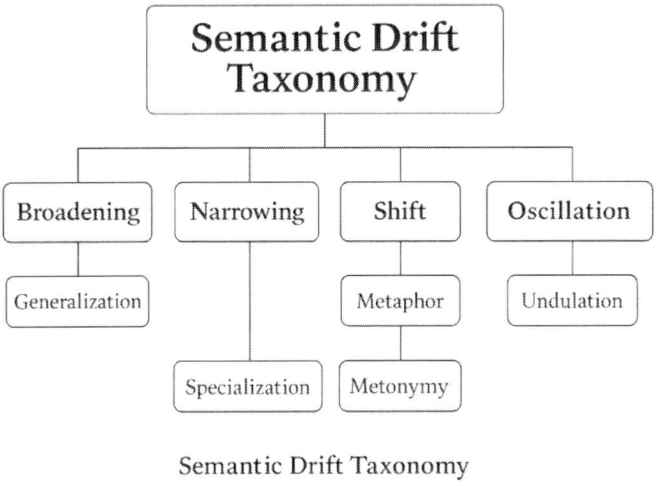

Figure 4.2 Semantic drift taxonomy.

Chapters 9 and 14 extend this into tools, governance workflows, and automation models that embed semantics directly into the data stack.

6. Embedding Semantics in the Stack

Semantic alignment cannot be something teams remember to do after building pipelines or dashboards. It must be designed into the stack itself. Meaning has to travel with the data; from source to consumption not live in slide decks, tribal memory, or static glossaries no one reads.

This is not just a philosophical preference. It is a scalability requirement. If meaning does not scale with systems, teams, and domains, inconsistency will.

The Modern Semantic Stack

The good news: organizations don't need entirely new tools.
They need to use existing layers of the data stack more intentionally.

1. Data Modeling Layer

Embed meaning at schema definition time:

- Use naming standards and conceptual modeling (dbt, ERDs).
- Tag entities and attributes with semantic markers (e.g., domain:provider, metric_type:retention, status_category).

This shifts data from *labeled storage → legible concepts.*

2. Data Contracts

Treat data contracts as semantic APIs, not just schema validators.

- Include value constraints, allowed states, and definitions; not only field types.
- Example: provider_status should assert allowed lifecycle states (active, suspended, terminated), not just VARCHAR.

Contracts become *intent*, not just *format.*

3. Metadata & Glossaries

Glossaries and catalogs only matter if they are integrated into daily workflows.

- Sync glossary definitions into dbt descriptions, dashboard tooltips, warehouse column comments.
- Make meaning *visible at the point of use*, not hidden behind another login.

A glossary no one sees is not governance; it is shelfware.

4. Transformation & Testing Layer

Semantic tests must be enforced in CI/CD not discovered by analysts later:

- If revenue should never be negative → assert it.
- If churned users must have inactivity > 90 days → assert it.

Tools: dbt tests, Great Expectations, Soda, PyDantic, semantic assertions in Airflow/Databricks.

Semantic quality should break the build, not the business.

5. Consumption Layer (BI & ML)

Meaning must survive the last mile:

- Dashboards should display glossary-linked definitions.
- Metrics in BI tools should map to the same semantic layer used in transformations.
- ML feature stores should store not only values, but meaning and lineage.

A metric that is trusted in a dashboard must be trusted in a model.

Example: Semantic Propagation in Action

A healthcare network tracks provider engagement:

Layer	What Happens
Modeling	provider_type is defined with allowed categories: primary_care, specialist, telehealth
Data Contract	Enforces only approved categories can be published
Transformations	dbt attaches glossary link + marks it a core domain dimension
Testing	Great Expectations validates no invalid provider types
Consumption	Dashboards automatically display definition tooltips; ML models inherit lineage context

From ingestion to insight, meaning is carried, validated, and communicated.

Design Principles for Embedding Semantics

To make semantics durable, adopt these design principles:

Principle	Meaning
Make meaning machine-readable	Encode semantics in metadata, tags, and contracts.
Version meaning like code	If definitions change, version them intentionally.

Surface context where decisions happen	In dashboards, notebooks, and APIs—not separate documents.
Bind producers to meaning	Data producers must define semantics, not just structure.

Governance becomes design, not oversight.

From Governance → Embedded Intelligence

This approach is not bureaucracy. It is how we prevent confusion from returning. A semantically aware stack doesn't just move data. It moves shared understanding.

And shared understanding is what makes data:

- Trustworthy
- Reusable
- Decision-ready

This is how organizations scale clarity not just pipelines.

If clarity begins with definition, resilience begins with structure; the foundation of Master and Reference Data.

CHAPTER 5

Foundations First: The Role of Master and Reference Data

"To speak is to fall into tautology. This world is the work of a god who is a librarian." - Jorge Luis Borges

Beneath every data system lies a quiet scaffolding of meaning — names, codes, and categories that let information make sense across contexts. This is the domain of master and reference data: not back-office hygiene, but the shared vocabulary that allows systems to interoperate, metrics to hold meaning, and decisions to scale without distortion.

Even the most advanced programs crumble without unified master records or harmonized code sets. Beneath the motion of pipelines and dashboards, something deeper holds an organization together, an invisible structure of definitions and relationships. It is the quiet architecture of trust.

These hidden structures (names, definitions, categories, and codes) are the silent agreements that let systems recognize the same thing in different places. They don't describe activity; they define reality. When these semantic anchors drift, systems don't fail noisily; they decay quietly. The loss is conceptual, and therefore harder to detect, but its impact is profound: trust erodes long before any error surfaces.

Master and reference data are how an organization remembers what it means. They form the enterprise's cognitive memory, ensuring that what *"customer"* or *"product"* means in one system aligns with its meaning in another. Without this alignment, data still flows, but meaning fractures; dashboards diverge, models confuse, and accountability fades.

This chapter reframes Master Data Management (MDM) and Reference Data Management (RDM) not as legacy governance exercises but as the semantic foundation of coherence in a distributed world. We explore what "good" looks like from golden-record stewardship and embedded metadata to governed vocabularies that allow systems to think and evolve together.

When these foundations weaken, misalignment spreads invisibly across systems until it surfaces as contradiction.
Consider the following real-world breakdown.

Failure Case Study: The EdTech Semantic Crisis

"What's our student dropout rate across regions?"

That was the question posed to the executive team of an international education technology company. They had invested in AI dashboards that tracked regional engagement trends. The charts looked promising until deeper inspection revealed misalignment.

The Breakdown:

Region	"Dropout" Definition
India	No login for 14 days
Brazil	No assignment submissions
U.S.	Decline in quiz scores over 3 tests

The "dropout" metric appeared on a global dashboard. But the executive summary masked semantic divergence.

Consequences:

- The U.S. showed a spike in dropouts, driven by test scores
- India appeared stable but masked silent disengagement
- Brazil was flagged erroneously as critical

What looked like regional trend variance was actually definition variance.

And the root cause? No shared master definition of student engagement, and no controlled reference for dropout condition.

Defining the Two Pillars

1. What is Master Data?

"Master data is the glue that binds your systems and the fault line where they often split." — Enterprise Data Strategist

Master data represents the core business entities that define the fundamental nouns of an organization: customers, products, suppliers, locations, employees. These entities are not isolated to a single system or team. They surface everywhere across operations, reporting, compliance, analytics, and machine learning.

Unlike transactional data (purchases, claims, visits), which captures events, master data describes the things those events refer to. It carries identity, history, and context, all of which require governance.

Small Change, Big Shift

A common misconception is that master data is "slow-moving" or "static." It may change less frequently than transactional data, but when it does, the impact cascades:

- A customer updates their legal name → billing, support history, audit logs shift
- A product is deprecated → recommendation logic and inventory forecasts adjust
- A provider's credentials change → regulatory filings must reflect it
- A facility relocates → logistics, zoning, tax mapping must realign

Every change to master data is a semantic event. And when unmanaged, these shifts ripple outward, quietly reshaping meaning across the system.

Lifecycle of Master Data Entities

Each master entity follows a lifecycle that crosses boundaries of tools, teams, and processes. For example:

Lifecycle Stage	System(s) Involved	Risk if Misaligned
Onboarded	CRM, Identity Provider	Duplicate records, unverified attributes
Activated	Billing, Support, Analytics	Inconsistent flags, undefined "active" state
Interacted	Product logs, Engagement system	Mislinked events, broken attribution

Modified	Customer portal, Admin tools	Stale references, compliance violations
Retired / Deleted	GDPR engine, Archival system	Orphaned records, reporting leakage

Each stage introduces a semantic boundary; who defines it, who validates it, who maintains continuity across versions?

Cross-Domain Complexity

In most enterprises, master data doesn't live in one place, it's duplicated and reinterpreted:

- **CRM (Salesforce):** relationships and engagement
- **ERP (SAP):** financial and operational attributes
- **Data warehouse:** reporting and analytics structures
- **Operational systems:** speed and specificity

Each domain sees *"Customer"* or *"Product"* differently.
Without a shared anchor, these differences aren't resolved, they're amplified.

What Happens Without It

Lack of MDM doesn't cause immediate failure. It causes slow semantic decay:

- Duplicate customers → inflated counts and misguided personalization
- SKU inconsistencies → fulfillment and billing errors
- Vendor mismatches → procurement and risk blind spots

- No versioning → regulatory and audit failures

Analysts become archaeologists, excavating logs and mappings to recover context that should have been defined once, clearly. Even the most modern cloud stack collapses into contradiction when identity is ambiguous.

Dashboards diverge. Models confuse. Trust erodes.

Without a shared understanding of core entities, every insight is built on semantic quicksand.

What Master Data Enables

When mastered effectively, these entities create strategic leverage:

- Seamless data interoperability
- Reliable and comparable metrics
- AI models trained on stable entity definitions
- Regulatory compliance with traceable lineage
- Meaningful 360-degree views across touchpoints

In an AI-driven era, master data is what grounds the machine in reality.

2. What Is Reference Data?

"It's just a list of values until one of them changes and breaks 42 reports."
— Data Governance Lead

Reference data is often dismissed as "just a lookup table," a static list in a spreadsheet or a dropdown hardcoded into an application. But reference data is far more than that. It is a semantic switchboard, the layer that translates raw values into meaning, enables consistent classification, and connects systems, domains, and external ecosystems.

Reference data consists of controlled vocabularies, enumerated lists, and classification schemes that constrain or describe attributes in a structured way.

It shows up everywhere:

- Dropdowns in user interfaces
- Filter criteria in BI dashboards
- Condition checks in rule engines
- Input validation in APIs
- Labels in machine learning training data

It is small in volume, but outsized in influence. One misaligned code or unapproved value can derail logic, distort reporting, or create *silent divergence* across systems.

Common Types of Reference Data

Type	Example	Use Case
Code Sets	ISO Country Codes (US, IN, BR)	Internationalization, shipping
Statuses	(Pending, Approved, Rejected)	Workflow and business rules
Classifications	Product categories (A/B/C, Tier 1)	Pricing, analytics, segmentation
Mappings	Old→New system values (e.g., M→Male)	Migration, integration
Hierarchies	Org units, geography, risk levels	Aggregation, policy enforcement

Some are industry-standard (ICD-10, ISO), others are organizationally-defined and culturally embedded.

Master Data vs. Reference Data vs. Transactional Data

To fully grasp the importance of master data, it helps to place it in context with other data types:

Type	Definition	Example	Frequency	Governance Complexity
Master Data	Core business entities	Customer, Product, Location	Medium	High
Reference Data	Controlled vocabularies for attributes	Status codes, Country codes	Low	Medium
Transactional Data	Event logs and interactions	Orders, Claims, Page Visits	High	Context-driven

Master data defines the entities.

Reference data categorizes them.

Transactions record activity around them.

Reference Data Lifecycle and Governance

Reference data, like master data, has a lifecycle but it's often unmanaged.

Stage	Activity	Risk if Ignored
Definition	Values are proposed, named, and structured	Ambiguity, misinterpretation
Validation	Business/IT owners approve	Uncontrolled sprawl
Distribution	Values are shared via APIs, files, UIs	Version mismatch across systems
Consumption	Used in rules, models, reports	Filter errors, label misalignment
Deprecation	Retired values tracked but not deleted	Historical misclassification, data loss

When this lifecycle is ignored, systems still run but they no longer mean the same things.

This is semantic drift. Failure Patterns in the Wild

Failure Patterns in the Wild

Mismanaged reference data rarely throws an error.
It generates something worse: confidence in incorrect results.

- Regulatory Failure
  Outdated ICD codes → millions in rejected healthcare claims.

- Broken Filters
  BI dashboards suddenly show "Unknown" as the fastest-growing segment → because one new code never made it to the report layer.

- Model Degradation
  Label values changed from (0,1) to (Inactive,Active) → model accuracy collapses silently.

- Silent Joins
  "EMEA" renamed to "Europe-MEA" in one system only → regional performance trends no longer reconcile.

Nothing crashed. Everything drifted.

Reference Data as a First-Class Product

High-maturity organizations treat reference data as stewardship, not configuration.

Practice	Description
Central Registry	Single authoritative value store
Versioning + Lineage	Every change traced across time
Cross-System Distribution	APIs and sync pipelines enforce consistency
Mapping Tables	Legacy-to-modern translations are explicit
Validation Rules	Enforced in ingestion + transformation layers
Consumer Notifications	Downstream systems know when values change

This transforms reference data from a fragile spreadsheet into an integration backbone.

AI & Analytics: The Hidden Dependency

Reference data plays an *unusually large* role in ML:

Label leakage: Models learn code semantics instead of patterns

- Feature confusion: "Region" means different things in different domains
- Drift blindness: Category changes reshape meaning without reshaping schema
- The model did not change. The meaning did.

Reference data is the semantic fingerprint of the business. When it shifts, downstream interpretation shifts with it.

Reference Data in Architecture

Whether you're working in a modern data stack or legacy integration environment, reference data shows up in surprising places:

- In **data contracts**, where expected value sets are predefined
- In **dbt models**, as source constraints or test conditions
- In **catalogs and glossaries**, as part of column-level metadata
- In **data lakes**, as filter logic and partitioning schemes

A well-managed reference data service becomes a semantic API layer abstracting meaning and exposing classification as code.

Reference Data Done Right Unlocks

- Consistent filtering and aggregation across BI tools
- Seamless data sharing with partners, vendors, and regulators
- Explainable AI, where models can be audited based on stable codes

- Reliable data contracts with strict value enforcement
- Easier migrations, where mappings are clearly versioned

Don't Let Small Lists Break Big Systems

Reference data may be small. Its consequences are not.

- One changed code can flip a trend line
- One renamed label can distort an executive decision
- One missing mapping can stall an entire workflow

Reference data is the operational vocabulary of the enterprise.
It deserves rigor not a spreadsheet on someone's desktop.

The Failure Patterns in the Wild

When master or reference data is neglected, systems don't crash—they lose meaning. Reports show inconsistent totals, customer behavior appears contradictory, and AI models begin to under-perform with no obvious bugs in sight.

At a global logistics firm, mismatched product codes between procurement and shipping systems led to delays and billing errors—even though each system passed validation independently. In a national healthcare network, misaligned provider identifiers across insurance, credentialing, and scheduling resulted in missed reimbursements and regulatory scrutiny.

These are not technical glitches. They are semantic failures—the result of fragmented definitions and uncontrolled drift in the identity and classification of core entities.

In one retail machine learning pipeline, model accuracy collapsed not because the algorithm changed, but because a new reference label for "emerging customer segment" was introduced upstream without corresponding updates downstream. Meaning shifted, and the machine quietly learned the wrong thing.

Across sectors, the patterns repeat: misaligned identifiers, ambiguous categories, ungoverned mappings, conflicting rules. The outcome is always the same: erosion of trust, compounding data debt, and expensive remediation disguised as technical troubleshooting.

Common Pitfalls:

- Entity Confusion
  - Multiple definitions of "Customer," "Product," or "Provider"
  - Results in fragmented attribution, misaligned counts, and billing errors

- Unmanaged Reference Drift
  - One team uses *Gold*, another uses *GOLD_TIER*
  - Codes multiply and diverge
  - Joins fail, filters break, trends distort

- Inconsistent Hierarchies
  - Sales organizes regions by geography
  - Support organizes by language
  - Executive dashboards cannot aggregate consistently

- No Lineage or Impact Visibility
  - A change to *Region Code* silently impacts 200+ reports and models
  - No one sees the blast radius until after decisions are already made

What Good Looks Like

In organizations where master and reference data are handled well, the topic rarely surfaces because things just work. The success is quiet, but deliberate.

In mature environments:

- Core entities (Customer, Product, Provider) have a golden record traceable across systems.
- Reference values (Region, Risk Level, Status) are governed, versioned, and published through consistent interfaces.
- Business and technical teams share a semantic contract about what key entities mean.
- Data quality issues are caught at the boundary before they spread.
- Downstream systems evolve independently because meaning is stable.
- ML and reporting pipelines don't need hacks or overrides—semantic alignment eliminates rework.

Most importantly, good MDM/RDM does not slow teams down.
It removes friction providing a foundation of shared truth that enables teams to move faster with confidence.

Design Principles for Master & Reference Data Success

Principle	Implementation	Benefit
Authoritative Source	Use a master data hub or registry	Consistent identifiers across systems
Governed Reference Data	Centralized vocabulary management	Reduced duplication and drift

Semantic Contracts	Define entity structure business meaning	Machine-readable context and control
Versioning Lifecycle	Track changes over time	Enables rollback, audit, and trust
Cross-Domain Stewardship	Data owners from multiple business units	Improves adoption, reduces blind spots

5. Aligning MDM/RDM with Modern Data Practices

Master Data Management (MDM) and Reference Data Management (RDM) are often associated with centralized, heavyweight governance platforms. But today's data landscape is anything but centralized. Distributed systems, domain-aligned teams, real-time pipelines, reverse ETL, feature stores, and AI workflows now define enterprise architectures.

To remain relevant, MDM and RDM must evolve from static registries to living, federated, interoperable semantic services, embedded directly into the modern stack rather than bolted on after the fact.

This isn't about discarding foundational principles.
It's about adapting them to velocity, scale, and decentralization without sacrificing meaning.

The Modern Stack: Where MDM/RDM Must Integrate

Let's look at where MDM and RDM now intersect with modern tools and practices:

Modern Practice	MDM/RDM Role
Feature Stores	Require stable master entity resolution for consistent feature lookup
Reverse ETL	Pushes product/customer IDs downstream; if keys don't match, context breaks
Event Streams (Kafka, Pulsar)	Master data helps enrich events in motion; reference data categorizes behavior
AI/ML Pipelines	Labels often derived from reference values; poor versioning causes drift
Data Products	Need productized entities with clear contracts and vocabularies
Data Mesh / Domain Ownership	Local ownership of master data, with federated governance of reference terms
Compliance-as-Code	Requires traceable mappings and value validation across data assets

MDM and RDM are no longer side systems. They are now inline semantic infrastructure.

Failure When Misaligned: A Real-World Composite

A large retail platform launched a real-time personalization engine based on user behavior, enriched with location and loyalty data.

But the underlying semantics weren't aligned:

- "Premium customer" meant different things in loyalty vs. marketing
- Zip code mappings drifted between warehouse and personalization engines
- Product variants weren't reconciled in the MDM and appeared as duplicates downstream

The model responded accordingly:

- Low-value users were over-targeted
- High-value users were deprioritized
- Regional attribution became misleading

The problem wasn't the algorithm. It was the meaning.

The fix was not retraining. It was semantic reconciliation.

AI Is Not Semantically Self-Healing

Modern AI workflows move fast—but they cannot correct conceptual misalignment:

- LLMs may hallucinate missing definitions, but they cannot detect conflicting ones
- Embeddings encode patterns, but depend on stable, consistent labels
- Monitoring frameworks detect anomalies, but not the semantic cause behind them

AI can scale insight. It cannot restore meaning after it is lost.

Design Patterns That Work in the Modern Stack

To embed MDM and RDM into today's infrastructure, organizations are moving toward modular, API-driven, and domain-aligned patterns.

MDM/RDM in Modern Architectures: Best Practices

Practice	Description
Semantic APIs	Expose master entities and reference lists via APIs for consumption
Data Contracts with Valid Sets	Define and enforce acceptable values, codes, and relationships upfront
CI/CD-Validated Reference Sets	Embed RDM checks into pipeline testing (e.g., dbt tests, Great Expectations)
Lineage-Aware MDM Stores	Track where entity definitions are used across the stack
Federated Stewardship Models	Allow domain teams to manage master entities while syncing global rules
Time-Versioned Reference Tables	Retain historical context and allow temporal queries for auditability

This shifts governance from policing to embedded reliability—trust enforced by design, not meetings.

Striking the Balance: Local Agility, Global Consistency

Modern data cultures must hold two truths at once:

- Teams need autonomy to move fast
- The organization needs shared meaning to move coherently

The solution is not complete centralization or complete federation, but layered semantics:

- Master entities are globally identified but locally enriched
- Reference values are centrally curated but domain-extensible
- Mapping tables mediate legacy vs. modern semantics
- Contracts and lineage ensure traceable interoperability

When this alignment holds, you don't just scale data. You scale understanding.

What Alignment Enables

- Model governance at machine scale
- Faster onboarding of new systems with shared vocabularies
- Audit-ready data pipelines with traceable reference lineage
- True data productization with stable entity interfaces
- Semantic resilience even as teams, tools, and architectures evolve

MDM/RDM Integration in the Modern Stack

1. Source Systems

- Correctly shown as the origin of both entity data (e.g., providers, patients) and code values (e.g., gender, specialties, regions).
- Systems like EHRs, ERPs, CRMs often feed both MDM and RDM layers.

2. Master Data Management Hub

- Properly includes:
  - Golden Record Creation – essential for deduplication, survivorship, and identity resolution.
  - Entity Matching & Hierarchy Management – foundational MDM services.
- Clearly feeds downstream systems and is governed at the semantic level.

3. Reference Data Management Store

- Accurate inclusion of:
  - Controlled Vocabularies & Domain Codes
  - Versioned Glossaries
  - Code Management APIs

- Indicates governed, stable, and versioned classifications feeding both MDM and analytics.

4. Metadata & Governance Layer

- Correctly shown as an overlay that supports:
  - Stewardship
  - Glossary Ownership
  - Lineage & Change Logs

- This is what enables trust at scale—not just technical success.

5. Semantic-Aware ETL / Pipelines

- The diagram implies that both MDM and RDM outputs are semantically enriched before landing in consumption layers—this is a key trust-preserving move.

6. Consumption Layer (BI, ML, APIs)

- Accurate depiction of consumers:
  - o BI tools using clean dimensions
  - o ML models needing canonical entities and consistent classifications
  - o Operational systems querying via APIs

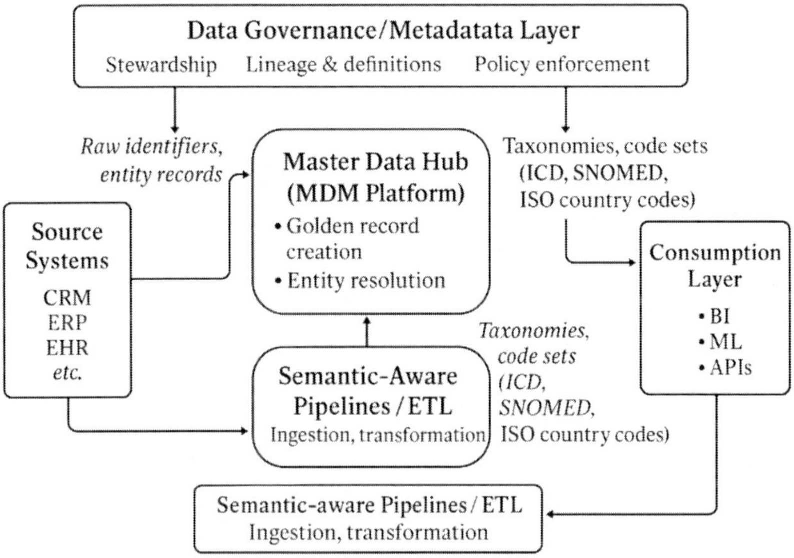

Figure 5.1 MDM hub with semantic-aware pipelines and a governance/metadata layer.

A Modern Stack Without Meaning Is Just Motion

No amount of data wrangling, cloud spend, or machine learning can fix semantic misalignment. The fastest pipeline still delivers garbage if the codes are wrong. The most scalable AI model still fails if it can't rely on stable definitions.

To future-proof your architecture, align your semantics. Modern data requires modern trust and trust starts with shared foundations.

6. Master and Reference Data Aren't Legacy: They're Strategic

Master Data Done Right Powers:

- Real-time personalization and customer experience
- Entity-level audit trails across systems
- GDPR/right-to-be-forgotten workflows
- Cross-system fraud and anomaly detection

Reference Data Done Right Enables:

- Consistent filtering and aggregation across BI tools
- Seamless interoperability with partners and regulators
- Shared trust in metrics across teams and functions

The best organizations don't treat MDM and RDM as hygiene or cleanup work. They treat them as first-class products in the data ecosystem; designed, governed, and evolved with intent.

Conclusion: In the end, most data failures are semantic failures.

- MDM clarifies *what* the organization is talking about.
- RDM clarifies *how* it is described and classified.

Without these foundations, systems may still run, dashboards may still refresh, and models may still predict but no one can be certain they mean the same thing. And no amount of engineering can compensate for confusion at the conceptual layer.

The most effective way to future-proof your data practice is not by buying more tools or moving faster but by grounding the organization in shared understanding.

To make any of this work, we must ground our systems in something deeper: a shared model of what our data means.

Modern Semantic Data Modeling

Most organizations still treat data modeling as an engineering step; an arrangement of tables optimized for pipelines, storage, or performance. But modern data modeling is no longer about shapes. It's about *semantics*: the shared language an organization uses to describe how its world works. A model succeeds not when it is technically elegant, but when anyone—analyst, engineer, product lead—can look at it and immediately understand what the data *means*.

Semantic modeling begins with concepts rather than columns. It asks simple but powerful questions:
What are the core entities we talk about? How do they relate? What does each concept represent, and what does it not?
By making these distinctions explicit, the model becomes more than a map of data. It becomes a map of meaning.

In this approach, definitions, reference values, and business rules aren't "supporting documentation". They are first-class components of the model itself. The glossary, the contracts, the code sets, the hierarchies: all of these are part of the semantic layer that ensures every downstream system—BI, ML, operational workflows—interprets data the same way. When a model embeds meaning, it eliminates the quiet ambiguities that otherwise lead to drift, rework, and mistrust.

A modern semantic model also reflects how organizations think, not just how they store. It prioritizes conceptual clarity before logical design, ensuring the structure follows the business, not the other way around. Entities are connected through meaningful relationships; who owns whom, who depends on what, and how events change state over time.

These relationships anchor the entire ecosystem, making lineage visible and interpretation intuitive.

The value of this approach becomes obvious in practice:

- New hires onboard faster because the model mirrors real-world language.
- Governance becomes lighter because meaning is explicit rather than inferred.
- Metrics and KPIs stabilize because their logic is grounded in shared concepts.
- AI models improve because their features align with verified semantics, not accidental patterns in the data.

As systems grow and architectures shift, the semantic model becomes the layer that endures; a source of truth that transcends tools, schemas, and platforms. Pipelines may change, storage layers may migrate, but the organization's understanding of itself must not.

A modern semantic data model preserves that understanding. It is the anchor that keeps meaning stable as everything else evolves.

CHAPTER 6

The Data Lifecycle: Meaning in Motion

"Data ages like milk, not wine."
— Unknown

In the previous chapters, we explored the semantic nature of data and the cultural foundations of ownership. We now shift to how data *evolves*—how meaning is preserved, altered, or lost as data moves through systems.

In early 2023, a fintech company deployed a real-time fraud detection model trained on historical transactions. It performed well in testing, but two months after launch, false positive rates spiked by 38%. Infrastructure was stable. Pipelines were healthy. The model hadn't changed.

The root cause was a quiet schema update upstream. A field called transaction_origin received new categories like VirtualCard and P2PTransfer—values the model had never seen. The pipeline didn't break. The model simply misinterpreted them.

Thousands of legitimate transactions were declined. Customer trust suffered. Risk teams lost confidence. This wasn't a bug; it was a lifecycle failure.

Data doesn't sit still; it moves, mutates, and sometimes decays. Every dataset travels a lifecycle: **collection → storage → transformation → consumption → archival → lineage.**

At each stage, meaning can be clarified, preserved, or quietly lost. Reliable systems aren't built by optimizing individual stages. They're built through lifecycle awareness, an understanding that meaning must remain traceable across every transition.

Data Doesn't Just Exist, It Evolves

Data is often treated as static, something that either exists or doesn't. In practice, data behaves more like a living artifact. It changes as systems, users, and assumptions change.

Every useful dataset undergoes a lifecycle. At each stage:

- Context can be preserved or lost
- Assumptions can be made explicit or buried
- Meaning can be aligned or drift silently

Most organizations focus on the visible end of the cycle: dashboards, reports, and models. But the quality of those outputs is determined long before consumption. Trust is either designed in or eroded upstream.

Data does not stand still. It moves through a living cycle of collection, storage, transformation, consumption, and archival. Each stage carries forward not just content but *context*; the meaning that makes data usable and trustworthy over time.

Each phase's design determines how AI systems later infer, adapt, and reason.

This chapter walks through the six phases of the data lifecycle and how to design each for resilience, clarity, and traceability. The lifecycle is not a straight line. It is a loop. Meaning must be continuously renewed.

The Data Lifecycle Wheel

Each phase introduces risks that compound across the cycle. Ignoring any phase breaks trust, context, or usability.

Each phase shapes how meaning travels through the system. We begin where every journey starts: collection.

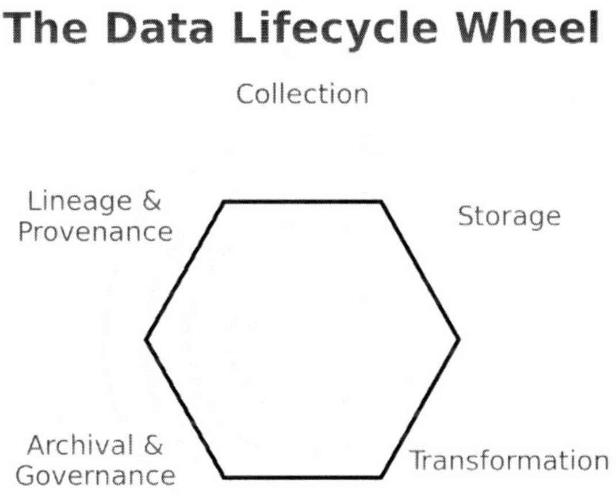

Figure 6.1 The Data Lifecycle Wheel across the full data loop.

Section 1: Collection — Data Starts Dirty or Incomplete

The lifecycle begins at the point of collection: logs, sensors, databases, web forms, APIs. This is where data is born and where its meaning is most vulnerable.

A common misconception is that *raw data is objective*. In reality, collection is shaped by human decisions: what to capture, what to ignore, how to format it, and under what constraints. Meaning is either preserved or distorted before data ever enters a pipeline.

Even before storage, data quality is influenced by:

- Device limitations (precision, sampling rates, default values)
- API contracts that omit contextual fields
- Form designs that bias or restrict user input
- Logging conventions that vary across teams or services

Common Weaknesses at Collection

- Missing or inconsistent timestamps (or time zones)
- Lack of unit representation (e.g., °F vs. °C)
- Null or empty-string defaults with no semantic reason
- Placeholder device values (e.g., -9999, UNKNOWN, 0)
- Logs missing application, environment, or request context

Example: An IoT system records temperature readings such as 72.4 but omits units, sampling frequency, and sensor location.
Technically valid. Semantically meaningless. That value cannot be reliably used in dashboards, ML features, or compliance audits.

Metadata is Not Auxiliary — It is the Data

To interpret a value, we must know:

- **Who** captured it (system, service, user)
- **When** it was captured (with time zone and clock accuracy)
- **Where** it originated (physical or logical source)
- **How** it was generated (method, trigger, device, or workflow)

Without this context, meaning collapses.

Key Practices

- Capture metadata alongside primary data (structured event/log formats)
- Adopt shared schemas for telemetry (e.g., OpenTelemetry, JSON Schema, Avro)
- Validate and enrich data at the point of entry, not downstream
- Quarantine, rather than silently accept, records missing required context

Extended Example: A customer feedback widget collects free-text input but does not store locale, login state, or page context. Months later, analysts attempt to correlate sentiment with geography and purchase behavior, but the contextual bridge is gone.
The data wasn't "low quality." It was *context-blind.* Once context is lost, no amount of downstream enrichment can fully restore the original meaning.

Design Principle: If context isn't captured at collection, it usually cannot be recovered. Data collection is not just about recording values; it is about preserving meaning. Every downstream decision inherits the assumptions made here.

Section 2: Storage — Structure Signals Intent

Once data is collected, often imperfectly, it must be stored. And storage is never just about persistence. The way data is stored signals assumptions about how it will be accessed, shared, and used.

Storage is not neutral. Schemas, formats, and physical locations encode intent. Transactional databases optimize for small, frequent updates. Analytical warehouses optimize for large, complex queries. Cloud object storage optimizes for durability. Cold archives optimize for cost.

How data is stored shapes what it can become next.

Key Storage Decisions

- **Normalized vs. Denormalized Structures**
  - Normalization preserves referential integrity and simplifies updates.
  - Denormalization improves read performance and reduces join complexity in analytics.

- **File Format**
  - CSV/JSON are human-friendly but loosely typed and inefficient.
  - Parquet/Avro provide strong typing, compression, and columnar access, ideal for analytical workloads.

- **Partitioning and Indexing**
  - Partitioning governs scan efficiency.
  - Indexing accelerates queries but increases write overhead.

- **Hot vs. Cold Storage Tiers**
  - Hot storage supports real-time access at higher cost.
  - Cold and archival storage reduce cost but slow retrieval.

Example: An analytics team exports daily data from an OLTP system. In the warehouse, analysts repeatedly re-join normalized tables to reconstruct customer purchase views. The result: unnecessary friction caused by a mismatch between source storage and analytical consumption needs.

Extended Considerations

- **Schema Evolution:** Can field types change without breaking consumers?
- **Lineage Support:** Can storage emit version and update history?

- **Access & Security:** Does the format enable row-level or column-level control?

Common Storage Pitfalls

- Treating the data lake as a dumping ground with no schemas or conventions
- Retaining legacy schemas that reflect outdated business logic
- Optimizing for writes at the expense of analytical usability
- Storing core datasets in semi-structured formats with no enforcement

Section 3: Logic, Lost in Transformation

Once data is stored, it rarely remains in its original form. It is cleaned, enriched, reshaped, aggregated, and joined; often repeatedly and by different teams.

This is the stage where business meaning becomes embedded in pipelines, but also where that meaning can become fragmented and invisible. Every transformation is an interpretation.

Whenever a field is filtered, mapped, recast, or derived, someone is deciding what the data means—whether explicitly (in dbt, SQL, or ETL logic) or implicitly (through dashboard filters or model features). When these decisions are not documented or governed, they become silent sources of semantic drift.

Transformation is also where semantic layering begins.

Small changes (like renaming status_code to is_active) can change interpretation. Complex derived fields such as *adjusted revenue* or *churn risk* encode entire belief systems about how the business works.

If these layers are not visible, meaning becomes implicit, tribal, and fragile.

Common Issues in Transformation

- Business logic duplicated across pipelines, dashboards, and applications
- Derived fields and KPIs defined differently across teams
- Logic embedded in code but disconnected from business context
- Silent breakage when upstream assumptions change

Example: An e-commerce company defines "active users" in three places:

- Login frequency (dbt)
- Recent purchases (dashboard filter)
- Engagement score (ML feature)

Leadership sees conflicting reports. Analysts reconcile manually. Data trust collapses. The problem is not the metric; it is the *unshared meaning* behind it.

Transformation Anti-Patterns

- Hardcoding business definitions inside SQL/Python with no documentation
- ETL pipelines that encode hundreds of decisions with no explanation for why
- Refactoring models without semantic versioning or impact analysis

Risks Introduced

- Hidden dependencies make pipelines brittle
- Debugging becomes slow and guess-based

- Downstream behaviors change silently
- Business trust erodes when the same question yields different answers

Best Practices

- Centralize and document core business logic in a shared semantic layer (dbt, LookML, MetricLayer, etc.)
- Treat transformations as code: versioned, tested, reviewed
- Align field and metric definitions with glossary and canonical models
- Validate outputs with domain owners so calculations reflect intent
- Add semantic assertions (e.g., Great Expectations) to ensure meaning-preserving behavior

Design Principle: Every transformation encodes meaning. Make that meaning explicit, traceable, and shared. Transformations should be transparent, versioned expressions of business understanding, not hidden logic buried in scripts.

What has been transformed must now be interpreted and that is where semantic risk multiplies.

Section 4: Consumption — Every Use Is an Interpretation

Once transformed, data is consumed by dashboards, APIs, spreadsheets, reports, notebooks, machine learning models, alerts, and executives. Consumption is where data turns into decisions. It is also where misunderstanding flourishes.

Every use of data is an interpretation.

Dashboards filter, models classify, spreadsheets aggregate: each carries assumptions about what the data means. When those assumptions are not shared, every consumer forms their own mental model.

Unaligned mental models are how semantic fragmentation enters the system.

Different Roles, Different Interpretations

- **Executives** seek clear KPIs tied to outcomes.
- **Analysts** explore raw data to validate conclusions.
- **Engineers** require stable, dependable APIs.
- **Data scientists** expect consistency between training and production.

Each persona requires not just access, but context. Without it, the same number can mean five different things to five different people.

Common Challenges at Consumption

- Users trust visualizations but not the logic behind them
- Metrics appear similar but differ due to hidden filters or joins
- No data contracts, so downstream consumers have no guarantees
- Upstream changes happen silently and without notification
- Lack of transparency into freshness, completeness, or lineage

Example: A churn model relies on a field called subscription_status. Last quarter, the transformation logic changed: paused users were re-categorized as inactive. The model's precision drops, but no alerts fire, and no one downstream is told.
The issue is not technical; it is semantic misalignment.

Hidden Risks in Consumption

- Business decisions based on misinterpreted metrics
- Models trained on outdated or redefined fields
- Reports compared without aligned definitions
- Silent lineage breakages that cannot be traced
- Teams duplicating analysis because trust has eroded

Best Practices for Reliable Consumption

- Link dashboards, queries, and models to versioned metric definitions
- Display lineage and context directly in BI tools and notebooks
- Monitor for semantic contract violations (e.g., null spikes, category drift)
- Teach consumers the assumptions and origin behind metrics
- Use a semantic layer to centralize business logic across tools
- Provide human-readable metric definitions within analytics interfaces

Design Principle: Make interpretation intentional, not accidental. Consumption should be the end of a traceable chain of meaning, not the point where meaning is reinvented by each user.

Every dashboard number has a shelf life. Governance decides when it expires and how gracefully.

Section 5: Archival & Governance — Forgetting by Design

Most data teams focus on collecting, transforming, and consuming data. Far fewer think seriously about how data should end its lifecycle. But archival and governance are not administrative afterthoughts. They are design responsibilities.

Archival is not just backup. It is the intentional process of deciding:

- What data to keep
- Where it should live
- How long it should be retained
- When it should be allowed to disappear

Governance ensures that data is handled according to its purpose, sensitivity, and obligations; legal, ethical, and operational.

Key Considerations for Archival

- **Retention policies:** What data must be retained? For how long? For what purpose?
- **Storage tiering:** When does data move from hot to warm to cold storage? What is the retrieval trade-off?
- **Indexability & discoverability:** Archived data should remain searchable for audit, investigation, and learning, not become a black hole.

Key Considerations for Governance

- **Compliance:** Regulations (GDPR, HIPAA, CCPA) require explicit handling of PII, consent revocation, erasure rights, and audit evidence.
- **Classification:** Data must be labeled with sensitivity level, domain ownership, and usage purpose.
- **Access control:** Row-level and column-level security prevent accidental or unauthorized exposure.

Example: A marketing dataset includes customer emails. A GDPR deletion request is executed, removing the customer's rows. Downstream dashboards break because a join depends on that customer ID.

The problem is not the deletion; it is that the data model was not designed to degrade gracefully.

Common Mistakes

- Deleting data without accounting for downstream dependencies
- Archiving data without metadata, making it effectively unusable
- Applying retention rules inconsistently across dev, staging, and prod
- Treating archival as a storage task instead of a lifecycle decision

Best Practices

- Automate retention enforcement with lineage-aware data tooling
- Use soft-deletion or anonymization when pure deletion compromises referential integrity
- Introduce governance checkpoints at ingestion, transformation, and publication
- Version and document retention and access policies just like code

Design Principle: Deletion is not the opposite of design. It is part of it. Thoughtful archival and governance ensure data remains trustworthy, compliant, and usable throughout its entire lifecycle.

Metadata loss compounds error across human and machine decisions. Whether data is kept or deleted, it must be traceable. That's where lineage and provenance complete the lifecycle.

Section 6: Lineage & Provenance — Traceable Trust

Trust in data is not built on accuracy or availability alone. It is built on traceability.

Teams must be able to answer a simple but powerful question:

Where did this data come from, and what happened to it along the way?

Lineage describes the flow of data across systems: its origins, the transformations applied, and where it ultimately lands. Provenance provides the contextual metadata: who changed it, when, and why.

Together, lineage and provenance provide transparency, accountability, and operational resilience.

Why Lineage Matters

- Debug failures and anomalies quickly by tracing upstream changes
- Perform impact analysis before modifying schemas or logic
- Support compliance, auditability, and reproducibility
- Increase analyst confidence through explainability

With vs. Without Lineage

Aspect	**With Lineage**	**Without Lineage**
Metric Breaks	Root cause identified in minutes	Days of guesswork
Upstream Changes	Impact understood before deployment	Silent downstream failures
Compliance Audits	Versioned and explainable	Manual scramble and uncertainty
Analyst Confidence	High — results are traceable	Low — everything feels questionable

Example: A key marketing metric drops 40% overnight. The cause? A column was renamed in an upstream dbt model, breaking a join. The dashboard didn't alert users. No one noticed for days. Lineage would have surfaced the break the moment it occurred.

Common Lineage Use Cases

- Identifying which dashboards, ML models, or APIs depend on a given column
- Understanding full dependency graphs before deprecating assets
- Revealing undocumented transformations that introduce semantic drift

Best Practices

- Capture lineage automatically in orchestration and transformation tools (dbt, Airflow, Dagster)
- Use column-level lineage when possible—dataset-level is often too coarse
- Surface lineage and data contracts directly in BI tools so consumers can self-serve trust
- Pair lineage with semantic contracts to detect breaking changes early

Provenance Adds Accountability

Lineage shows *what* happened. Provenance explains *why* it happened.

Key provenance questions:

- Who made the change?
- Why was the transformation introduced?
- When was the dataset last updated?

- Was the update successful, complete, and timely?

Design Principle: Data without traceability invites mistrust. Lineage and provenance are not engineering add-ons. They are trust infrastructure for the entire organization.

The Four Lifecycle Failure Modes

These are the recurring ways meaning breaks across the lifecycle.

Failure Mode	Symptom	Prevention Tactic
Context Loss	Ambiguous fields, unusable logs	Capture metadata early and consistently
Invisible Drift	Metrics change silently without warning	Lineage + data contracts + semantic validation tests
Logic Fragmentation	Conflicting KPIs across teams	Central semantic layer + glossary-aligned definitions
Ownership Gaps	Issues persist because no one is responsible	Assign and document accountable stewards

These failures are subtle because they do not always break pipelines. They break **meaning**.

Semantic Health Scorecard — Measuring Meaning at Scale

A data platform's maturity cannot be measured only by pipelines or uptime. Semantic clarity—how well meaning is defined, governed, and shared—is a core dimension of trust. Without shared meaning, even perfectly engineered systems produce unreliable insights.

Metric	Description	Target
% of glossary terms with assigned owners	Measures accountability for definitions	90%+
# of certified metrics in production dashboards	Indicates semantic governance adoption	Trending up
Contract test coverage rate	% of pipelines with semantic validation checks	80%+
Glossary usage in queries / lineage	Reflects real adoption of shared meaning	Increasing MoM
Time-to-Clarify (TTC)	Avg. time to resolve semantic ambiguity questions	< 48 hours

Tracking these metrics shows not just what the data says, but whether people can agree on what it **means**.

Quick Check: Where Are You Most Vulnerable?

Use these questions as a lightweight lifecycle assessment:

Phase	Key Question
Collection	Are time zones and units captured accurately?
Storage	Are schemas versioned and documented?
Transformation	Is business logic centralized and traceable?

Consumption	Do metrics have clear owners and definitions?
Archival	Are retention rules enforced automatically and consistently?
Lineage	Can every dashboard metric be traced to its source?

A failure in any single phase introduces semantic distortion that compounds downstream.

From Definition to Delivery — How Meaning Evolves

Data doesn't just move; it changes. At each stage in its lifecycle, meaning can be reinforced or lost. Organizations must treat meaning as a versioned, living artifact, not a static label. This requires feedback loops, semantic contracts, and governed evolution.

Stage	Semantic Activity	Risk Without Governance
Definition	Term is created, steward assigned, glossary entry added	Meaning starts incomplete or ambiguous
Transformation	ETL/ELT applies filters, joins, and calculations	Logic diverges from business intent
Modeling	Metrics/features are built using transformed fields	Proxy assumptions or misaligned features
Delivery	Dashboards / APIs expose the term	Visual misinterpretation or stale logic

Usage	Stakeholders act based on the term	Decisions diverge and trust erodes
Revision	Meaning is updated based on feedback or audit	Updates do not propagate downstream

The organizations that thrive are the ones that don't just manage data, they manage meaning in motion.

CHAPTER 7

Designing with Data at the Center

"If we have data, let's look at data. If all we have are opinions, let's go with mine."
— Jim Barksdale, former Netscape CEO

Modern organizations increasingly depend on data to make decisions, automate processes, and personalize experiences. Yet many still design systems as though data were a secondary artifact; a byproduct of code, not the purpose of the system itself. This chapter argues for the opposite: data is the enduring asset; code is the temporary scaffolding. System design must begin with data, not follow from it.

A large retailer once discovered two dashboards presenting different revenue figures to the executive team. Both were "correct" according to their respective pipelines, but derived from different interpretations of what counted as revenue. As discussed in Chapter 4, ambiguity masquerading as correctness is one of the most dangerous forms of misalignment. The issue was not technical failure but semantic disagreement embedded deep in the system.

To design reliable systems, organizations must start with agreement not just on logic, but on meaning.

From Code-Centric to Data-Centric Thinking

Traditional systems are designed with code as the center of gravity. Teams begin with:

- Workflows
- Services
- Endpoints
- UI behaviors

Only after implementation do they ask, "What data do we need?" and by then, the data model is constrained by the decisions already made.

But data persists far longer than code. Code is rewritten every few months. Data lives for years, sometimes decades, and feeds reporting, machine learning, compliance, personalization, and automation. As emphasized in Chapter 6, data evolves, its meaning must be guarded across time.

Data-centric design reverses the order of thinking:

1. Define the truth of the domain first
2. Then design services and behavior around it

This orientation requires that systems be built to record reliable facts before performing actions.

In a data-centric architecture, data must be:

- **Consistent** across services
- **Interpretable** by both humans and machines
- **Durable** across system and team changes

This shift influences how features are scoped, how ownership is assigned, how systems interoperate, and how trust is preserved.

The D-SILT Model of Data-Centric Design

This chapter introduces five principles that guide teams toward de-signing systems where data is the foundation. These principles shift architecture from reactive correction to intentional meaning design. Together, they ensure that the truths an organization depends on are defined explicitly, shared consistently, and preserved over time, not reconstructed after the fact. In other words, D-SILT is how systems learn to remember.

Principle	**Meaning**
D — Data First	Define entities and relationships before application logic
S — Schema as Contract	Treat schemas as stable, governed agreements
I — Interface by Data	Structure system boundaries around data, not RPC procedures
L — Logic-Tested (Test Like Code)	Test and validate meaning, not just shape
T — Trust through Discoverability	Make data findable, interpretable, and owned

Each principle builds on lessons from earlier chapters, but applies them directly to system and architecture design.

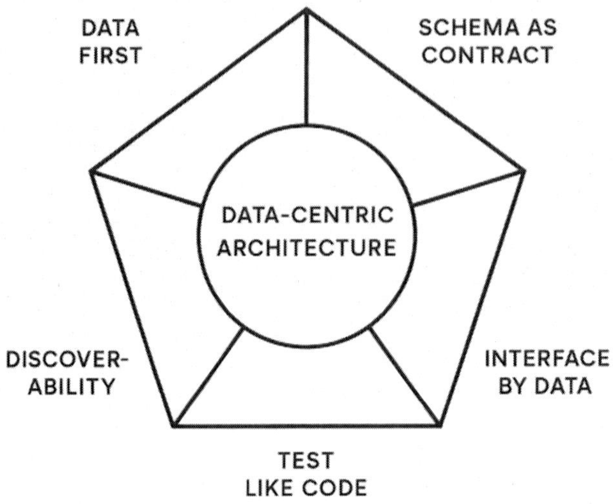

Figure 7.1 Data-centric architecture principles (D-SILT)

Principle 1: Design Data First

In many organizations, systems are designed around services and endpoints first. Teams sketch workflows, define APIs, and write business logic and only then derive data models to support those behaviors. The result is predictable: each system encodes its own version of core business entities. "Customer" in billing is not the same as "Customer" in CRM. "Order" in fulfillment is not the same as "Order" in analytics. The differences start small, then become systemic, and eventually expensive.

Data-first design reverses this sequence.

Before designing APIs, microservices, or feature logic, teams collaboratively define:

- The **core entities** that structure the domain (e.g., Customer, Product, Policy, Provider)

- The **attributes** that give them meaning (fields, data types, constraints, units)
- The **relationships** that bind them (hierarchies, cardinalities, ownership boundaries)
- The **domain language** people already use to describe them

This establishes a stable semantic backbone, a shared truth, before any code is written.

See Chapter 5 for how master and reference data provide the enterprise vocabulary that makes shared meaning possible.

Once these entities are defined, services and pipelines become expressions of the data, not competing interpretations of it.

Example: A team building subscription billing is tempted to start with endpoint flows (e.g., /createSubscription, /renewSubscription).
Instead, they begin by defining the Subscription entity itself:

Field	**Meaning**	**Owner**	**Constraints**
subscription_id	Unique business identifier	Billing	Immutable
status	Enum: active, paused, expired	Customer Ops	Must match RDM code set
start_date	When billing began	Finance	Must not be null
renewal_term	Monthly, annual, custom	Product	Must align with contract terms
currency	ISO 4217 code	Finance	Must match region price book

The definition is reviewed across Finance, Product, Customer Support, Analytics, and Engineering. Misunderstandings are surfaced early, not discovered months later during reconciliation or reporting failures.

Downstream systems inherit clarity, not ambiguity.

Why This Matters

When the data model comes first, every system is aligned to the same meaning. When the data model comes last, every system encodes its own interpretation.

This is not just modeling. It is organizational alignment.

Design Principle: If you don't define your data before writing code, your systems will encode assumptions instead of truth.

Data-first design ensures your architecture reflects how the business *actually works*, not how one implementation happened to express it.

Principle 2: Treat Schemas as Contracts

In software systems, interfaces define expectations. In data systems, schemas serve that same role but too often, they are treated as *internal implementation details*, rather than shared commitments.

A schema is a contract between a producer and a consumer. It specifies:

- What fields exist
- Their types, constraints, and allowable values
- The meaning those fields carry in the business
- The relationships to other entities and records

When treated as a contract, a schema removes ambiguity and establishes a stable semantic boundary between systems and teams.

When schemas function as contracts:

- Changes are reviewed, versioned, and communicated
- Downstream systems are notified of breaking changes
- Validation and testing are automated rather than ad-hoc
- Ownership is explicit, not assumed

See Chapter 5 for how master and reference data provide the vocabulary these schemas rely on.

Example: A streaming pipeline publishes customer events in Avro. Schema evolution rules are enforced: new fields must be additive and optional. When marketing_opt_in is introduced, consumers who don't yet use the field continue uninterrupted—no silent failures, no emergency rollbacks, no broken dashboards.

This is the difference between semantic stability and semantic drift.

Why This Matters

Schemas do more than define structure. They define meaning.

A field called status is useless unless the organization agrees:

- What values are allowed
- Who assigns them
- What lifecycle transitions are possible
- What each state implies

Without that clarity, two dashboards can tell two different stories from the exact same data.

This becomes even more critical in machine learning where misinterpreted fields lead to models that are *confidently wrong*. Chapter 14 returns to this point in the context of explainable and accountable AI.

Anti-Patterns

- Inferring schemas implicitly from sample data
- Renaming or retyping fields without communicating changes
- Storing critical data in free-form JSON blobs or nested payloads
- Relying on tribal knowledge, Slack threads, or dashboards for meaning

These patterns make systems fragile. They also push interpretation responsibilities onto consumers where inconsistency is guaranteed.

Best Practices

- Use schema registries (Confluent, Apicurio, Lake Formation) to enforce contracts and support discovery
- Apply backward-compatible schema evolution rules
- Include semantic metadata: field definitions, permissible values, units, links to glossary terms
- Version schemas intentionally not by accident
- Require peer review for schema changes just like application code

Design Principle: Treat every schema as a public API.

A schema change is not a low-level technical adjustment. It is a semantic event that affects how the organization understands itself. When schemas are treated as contracts, systems interoperate, teams stay aligned, and meaning scales.

Principle 3: Interface Through Data

Traditional service design starts with APIs: teams define endpoints, HTTP verbs, and request/response payloads. But in data-centric systems, the interface is not the endpoint. It is the data itself.

Interface-Through-Data means that shared data shapes (the semantic models of core business entities) form the primary contract between systems. APIs become transport mechanisms not the source of meaning.

Rather than designing getCustomerById() and then inferring what a *Customer* is, we define the Customer entity first; its fields, constraints, lifecycle states, and allowed relationships. The API simply exposes that model.

This prevents one team's "Customer" or "Order" object from silently diverging from another's: an issue discussed in Chapter 5 when core concepts lack semantic alignment.

Why This Matters

- **Data outlives services.** APIs change, get replaced, decomposed, re-versioned. Data models persist in storage, analytics, ML features, contracts, invoices, audit logs.
- **Meaning must be stable even when systems change.** If data models drift, reports, decision systems, and machine learning pipelines drift with them.
- **More consumers interact with data than with APIs.** Reverse ETL, event pipelines, BI models, semantic layers, notebooks; all depend on the *shape* of the data, not the endpoints that moved it.

Example: A microservice returns customer data as a loosely typed JSON response. Over time, different clients rely on different fields, and the service grows complex conditional branches. A single renaming breaks dashboards and ML workflows.

The team replaces this with a published, versioned Customer schema in a schema registry (Avro/Protobuf/GraphQL SDL). Clients bind to the schema not the endpoint. When new fields are added, downstream systems adapt predictably.

The API becomes simply a delivery mechanism.

Anti-Patterns to Avoid

- Endpoints whose payloads change without versioning
- "Helper" fields added ad-hoc for a single consuming system
- Free-form JSON blobs or nested maps with no authoritative meaning
- RPC-style interfaces that hide domain semantics behind procedural calls

These patterns bury meaning in code and make systems hard to reason about, scale, or govern.

Best Practices

Practice	Outcome
Publish schemas first, APIs second	Prevents semantic drift across teams
Use self-describing formats (Avro, Protobuf, GraphQL SDL)	Enables auto-documentation and validation
Register schemas and version them centrally	Supports evolution without breaking consumers
Link fields to glossary and master data definitions	Ensures business meaning travels with data

Design Principle: APIs are temporary. Data is durable.

Design your systems so that the *data model* is the interface not the routing layer that moves it. When teams interface through data, systems evolve without losing meaning. This is what allows organizations to scale coherently, not just quickly.

Principle 4: Test Data Like Code

In software engineering, testing is non-negotiable. We write unit tests, integration tests, regression tests, and wire them into CI/CD pipelines. We assume code will break unless proven otherwise.

Yet in many organizations, data is deployed without equivalent safeguards.

Pipelines silently fail. Dashboards quietly diverge. Models degrade slowly and invisibly. And because the failure modes are semantic rather than syntactic, they often surface only when trust has already been damaged.

If data is driving decisions, then testing data is as essential as testing code.

(See Chapter 6 for how meaning drifts silently when lifecycle monitoring is missing.)

Why Data Testing Matters

- **Schema validation** ensures producers adhere to shared expectations.
- **Null and range checks** catch missing or distorted values early.
- **Distribution and drift tests** detect subtle changes in meaning that do not break pipelines but do break decisions.
- **Freshness and latency checks** ensure data is timely enough to be trusted.

Data failures rarely look like crashes. They look like slowly diverging truth.

Example: A third-party vendor updates their export format. Half of the incoming transactions now arrive without customer_id.
Nothing breaks. Pipelines run. Dashboards load. Sales velocity appears to collapse overnight.

A single assertion, customer_id IS NOT NULL, would have caught the issue upstream.

Instead, the business discovers it in the board review.

Types of Data Tests

Test Type	What It Ensures	Examples / Tools
Schema Tests	Field presence, type correctness, enumerated values	dbt tests, Avro/Protobuf schema registry rules
Quality Tests	Completeness, uniqueness, valid ranges	Great Expectations, Soda
Freshness Tests	Data arrives when expected	Monte Carlo, Databand
Business Rule Tests	Domain meaning holds	Custom SQL assertions
Statistical Tests	No silent drift in distributions or features	Deequ, Evidently AI

Common Anti-Patterns

- Testing only transformation outputs not raw inputs.
- Silently discarding invalid records instead of surfacing alerts.
- Treating dashboards as quality gates instead of validation tools.
- Relying on manual checks ("looks right to me") as assurance.

These patterns allow errors to accumulate unseen.

Best Practices

- **Shift Left:** Validate data contracts in staging before production.
- **Automate:** Run tests on every pipeline execution and code merge.
- **Monitor:** Alert on anomalies, null spikes, and drift in production.
- **Collaborate:** Define data quality expectations with domain experts.
- **Expose Results:** Make testing status visible in catalogs and BI tools.

When test results are transparent, trust is earned, not assumed.

Design Principle: If you wouldn't ship untested code, don't ship untested data.

Trust is not a given. It is a tested property. A system can only be trusted if it is understandable. Discoverability determines whether data becomes knowledge or remains exhaust.

Principle 5: Build for Discoverability

A data model is only as valuable as it is *findable and understandable.*
In data-centric organizations, discoverability is not documentation, it is infrastructure. If people cannot locate the right dataset, trust its meaning, or understand how to use it responsibly, they will either:

- Rebuild the dataset themselves (redundancy), or
- Use the wrong dataset (misinterpretation).

Both are symptoms of *semantic opacity*, not technical failure.

Discoverability means:

- People know what data exists.

- They understand the meaning behind it.
- They know where it came from and how it should be used.
- They know who to ask when something is unclear.

If any of these is missing, trust collapses and the data platform fragments into local knowledge pockets and shadow pipelines.

(See *Chapter 3: Data Strategy and Ownership* for how ownership enables clarity and accountability.)

Why Discoverability Matters

- Reduces duplicated pipelines and one-off work.
- Empowers domain teams to self-serve responsibly.
- Promotes shared interpretation of key metrics and dimensions.
- Accelerates onboarding and cross-functional collaboration.
- Makes governance *practical*, not bureaucratic.

Elements of Discoverability

Element	Description
Searchable Catalog	A centralized inventory of available data assets with search and browsing capabilities.
Clear Glossary Terms	Standardized definitions of key business terms to ensure shared understanding across teams.
Lineage Tracing	The ability to trace data's origins, transformations, and movement across systems.
Column-Level Descriptions	Field-level explanations that clarify meaning, units, constraints, and intended use.

Owner Metadata	Clear assignment of data stewards or custodians responsible for quality and correctness.
Access Protocols	Rules governing who can access data and under what conditions, balancing security and usability.

Discoverability is not *just* tooling. It is tooling *plus* language *plus* ownership.

Example: A company implements a semantic layer where:

- Each metric links to its glossary definition.
- Each dataset lists an accountable owner.
- Each field includes description, type, and business meaning.
- Lineage diagrams show upstream systems and downstream consumers.

New analysts stop asking *"Where is the real customer table?"*

They already know. Analysis accelerates. Reconciliation work disappears. Leadership stops arguing over whose number is "correct.". Trust increases.

Anti-Patterns

- Data scattered across warehouses, BI tools, exports, and SaaS apps.
- Spreadsheets or dashboards acting as the "real" source of truth.
- Cryptic table and field names with no documented meaning.
- Analysts relying on oral tradition: *"Ask Priya, she knows what that field means."*

If meaning lives in people instead of systems, the organization cannot scale.

Best Practices

- Maintain a searchable, organization-wide catalog with lineage and ownership.
- Link datasets → glossary terms → semantic layer metrics.
- Embed documentation *at the point of use* (dashboards, notebooks, queries).
- Use certification signals (e.g., *Trusted*, *Deprecated*, *Experimental*).
- Apply role-based access control without hiding metadata visibility.

Documentation should be *ambient*, always visible where the data is used.

Design Principle: Discoverability fuels reuse. Data that cannot be found, understood, or trusted is functionally equivalent to data that does not.

Make every data product visible, interpretable, and accountable by default.

CHAPTER 8

Architectures That Preserve Meaning

"The greatest challenge in communication is the illusion that it has taken place."
— George Bernard Shaw

Design establishes meaning; architecture operationalizes it. Architecture is not merely about performance, durability, or scale. It is about whether meaning survives as data moves across systems, teams, and time.

In 2019, a large health insurer faced what looked like a catastrophic billing failure. An automated audit flagged a surge of claims marked *reversed* over ninety days, more than $80 million. Dashboards lit up. Executives panicked. Investigations began. Regulators were notified.

But the truth was simpler and more telling.

Nothing catastrophic had happened. The system was simply overwriting claim states in-place. The flag *reversed* did not mean a payment was undone, it meant an adjustment workflow had begun. Because the architecture stored only *current state* with no event history, no one could reconstruct intent. And because the data warehouse copied only the final state, every team interpreted the data differently:

- Compliance believed there was misconduct.

- Product assumed a system defect.
- Data science retrained fraud models with distorted inputs.

The problem was not the data. It was the architecture's failure to preserve meaning.

Most modern data failures are not failures of volume, scale, or latency. They are failures of *semantic integrity*.

This chapter examines architectural patterns that *protect* meaning, not just move data.

Why Architecture Must Follow Semantics

Traditional architecture emphasizes modularity, throughput, and separation of concerns. These are necessary qualities—but in data-driven environments, they are not sufficient. Architecture must also preserve:

- **Clarity** — what the data represents
- **Context** — why it changed
- **Continuity** — how meaning evolves over time

In application-centric architectures, data is a *byproduct* hidden behind service boundaries. But in data-centric architectures, data is the *interface.* It must be modeled explicitly, shared consistently, and governed intentionally.

Architecture becomes not only a technical discipline, but an epistemic one:
a framework for how knowledge is represented and retained across teams, systems, and time.

Why This Matters

- Without shared semantics, data becomes brittle and fragmented.
- Misinterpreted data produces misleading dashboards and flawed models.
- When architecture fails to encode meaning, integration becomes slow, manual, and error-prone.

This chapter explores structural patterns that maintain semantic alignment and sustain trust at scale. These are not just implementation choices—they are organizational commitments.

Five Architectural Patterns for Semantic Alignment

1. **Event-Driven, Not CRUD-Driven**
   Capture not just what changed, but why.

2. **Command–Query Responsibility Segregation (CQRS)**
   Separate the intent to act from the need to observe.

3. **Data Mesh Principles**
   Align ownership and meaning to the domain that knows it.

4. **Self-Describing Data**
   Embed structure and semantics directly in the data itself.

5. **Polyglot Persistence with Shared Semantics**
   Allow diverse storage technologies, anchored by common meaning.

Each of these patterns treats data not as output, but as a durable expression of business reality. They enable systems that do not merely process information, but *preserve* it.

Pattern 1: Event-Driven, Not CRUD-Driven

Most enterprise systems are built around CRUD (Create, Read, Update, Delete) operations. In this model, data is treated as a mutable object whose state is overwritten in place. While suitable for transactional processing, CRUD architectures erase context—they record *what* something is now, but not *how* or *why* it became that way.

Event-driven architecture takes the opposite view. It represents business activity as a stream of immutable events:

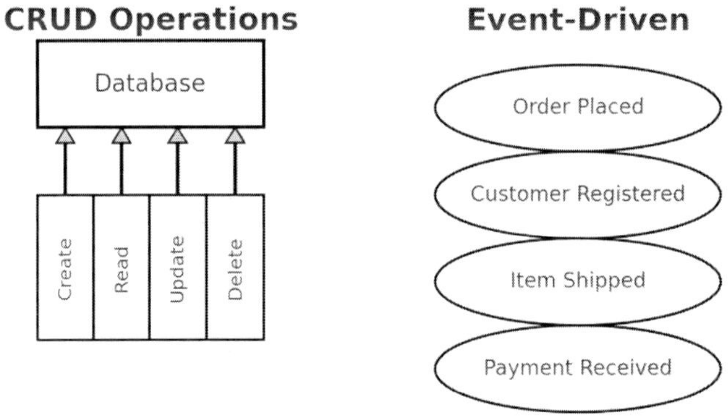

Figure 8.1 State-centric vs event-centric thinking.

These events capture intent, timing, and cause, preserving meaning rather than replacing it.

Why Events Matter

- Events are durable *facts of history*, not just snapshots of state.
- They reflect *business language*, not internal system mechanics.
- They allow systems to reconstruct *how meaning evolved over time.*
- They enable temporal and behavioral analytics that CRUD erases.

CRUD Model	Event-Driven Model
Overwrites current state	Appends new facts
Meaning is lost	Meaning accumulates
Hard to audit root cause	Traceable, replayable history
Low domain alignment	High semantic alignment

Example

In a CRUD system, updating a shipping address simply replaces a field. In an event-driven system, an AddressUpdated event records:

Field	Value
old_address	Previous address
new_address	Updated address
updated_by	User or system
timestamp	When the change occurred
reason	Why the change occurred

This preserves context for:

- Customer service scripts
- Fraud analysis
- Legal audit
- Machine learning feature derivation

Design Considerations

- Use immutable event logs (Kafka, Pulsar, EventBridge) as sources of truth.
- Define event schemas using domain language, not table fields.
- Version events explicitly—meaning evolves.
- Consumers should respond to events, not poll for state.

Common Pitfalls

- Emitting generic "CustomerUpdated" events with no semantic intent.
- Treating events as *messages* instead of *business facts*.
- Losing traceability because events are not stored permanently.

Design Principle: Model your architecture around what *happens*, not just what *is*.
State tells you the result. Events tell you the story.

Pattern 2: Command-Query Responsibility Segregation (CQRS)

In many systems, the same service model handles both **commands** (which *change* state) and **queries** (which *read* state). This creates contention, coupling, and conceptual blur: the model must serve two competing purposes.

CQRS separates these concerns.

- A command model validates and applies *intentful changes.*
- A query model provides read-optimized *representations* of state.

Why CQRS Matters in Semantic Systems

- Commands express business intent (e.g., "pause subscription").

- Queries reflect information needs (e.g., "show active customers").
- Each side can evolve independently with different schemas, stores, or performance profiles.

Benefits

- Clearer reasoning: *why* something changed is isolated from *how* it is read.
- Write-side schemas stay normalized and precise.
- Read-side schemas can be denormalized for analytics or UI without polluting domain models.
- Enables eventual consistency where appropriate, strengthening scale.

Example: In a commerce system, placing an order generates a command processed by the transactional write model. Meanwhile, customer-facing dashboards query a read model that is optimized for fast access and includes enriched order history, shipping status, and estimated delivery.

When Not to Use CQRS

CQRS adds complexity. It is not for simple CRUD applications.
Use it when:

- Domains are complex and evolve over time
- Read workloads and write workloads differ significantly
- Traceability or domain behavior correctness matters

Avoid it when the domain is simple, static, or low-scale.

Design Principle: Separate the intent to act from the need to know. Clarity of purpose leads to clarity of meaning.

Pattern 3: Data Mesh Principles

As organizations grow, centralized data platforms often become a bottleneck. A small platform team attempts to serve every analytics need for every domain. They maintain pipelines, quality expectations, dashboards, metric definitions, lineage, and more. Eventually, they are overwhelmed not because they lack skill, but because they lack *context.*

Data is inseparable from domain meaning. And meaning does not scale centrally.

Data Mesh addresses this by aligning data ownership with domain boundaries. Instead of funneling all data engineering through a shared central pipeline team, each domain produces and maintains its own data products with clear contracts, quality guarantees, and documentation.

Core Principles

1. **Domain Ownership**
   Data lives where knowledge lives. The teams closest to the business process maintain the data.

2. **Data as a Product**
   Data products have owners, support levels, documentation, versioning, and predictable behavior.

3. **Self-Serve Platform Infrastructure**
   A central platform provides shared capabilities — logging, storage, lineage, governance — without dictating meaning.

4. **Federated Governance**
   Standards are shared. Ownership is distributed. Semantic alignment is maintained collectively.

Example: A Payments team publishes a Transaction data product with:

- A stable schema & glossary links
- Quality checks and freshness SLAs
- Column-level lineage
- Version history and change notifications

Marketing uses this product to compute LTV and retention metrics without submitting tickets or reverse-engineering business logic.

Benefits

- Faster analytics iteration
- Less centralized backlog pressure
- Clear domain accountability
- Better semantic alignment across teams

Common Pitfalls

- Calling it "mesh" while keeping ownership centralized
- Domains publishing data without quality expectations
- Governance that is *optional* instead of *protocol-driven*

Design Principle: Meaning lives with the people who use it. Align ownership with domains, not technology tiers.

Pattern 4: Self-Describing Data

Self-Describing A dataset that requires tribal knowledge to interpret is not a usable dataset. Meaning shouldn't live in wiki pages, Slack threads, or the memories of senior analysts. When data is extracted, transformed, shared, or streamed across systems, it must *carry its meaning with it.*

Self-describing data embeds structure and semantics directly into the data itself.

Why This Matters

- Reduces dependence on manual interpretation
- Enables automation and reasoning across tools
- Accelerates onboarding and reuse
- Makes data resilient to personnel and system change

Forms of Self-Description

Format / Capability	What It Conveys
Avro / Parquet / ORC schemas	Field types, structure, metadata
Enumerated code sets	Allowed values with semantic meaning
JSON with $schema references	Validation + machine interpretation
Feature / metric stores	Versioned definitions with provenance

Example: A Parquet dataset storing machine learning features includes:

- Column descriptions and units
- Statistical distribution summaries
- Source lineage and quality checks

When the feature distribution shifts, downstream models detect the drift automatically.

Common Pitfalls

- Assuming *schema = meaning* (it is not)
- Embedding metadata but not versioning it
- Allowing semantics to drift across domains

Design Principle: If the data cannot explain itself, someone else will and they may guess wrong. Make meaning portable.

Pattern 5: Polyglot Persistence with Shared Semantics

Modern systems rarely rely on a single data store. Different workloads have different needs:

- transactional accuracy,
- analytical scale,
- search and retrieval speed,
- relationship traversal,
- or semi-structured flexibility.

This leads naturally to polyglot persistence using multiple storage technologies side by side:

- **Relational databases** for OLTP integrity
- **Columnar warehouses** for analytics
- **Document stores** for flexible records
- **Search indexes** for text retrieval
- **Graph databases** for networked relationships

This diversity is not a problem. Meaning divergence is.

If each system defines "Customer," "Order," or "Claim" differently, the organization begins to fracture semantically. Analytics teams spend more time reconciling differences than generating insights. Data scientists engineer features to *fix* mismatched meaning instead of modeling behavior. Integration becomes a translation exercise between similar-sounding but incompatible representations of the business.

Polyglot persistence is powerful but only if the semantics remain unified.

Shared Semantics: The Anchor Across Stores

Polyglot persistence works when storage diversity is bound together by a shared semantic layer, a set of canonical definitions and contracts that preserve meaning, regardless of how data is stored or optimized.

This layer may include:

- A **shared schema registry**
- A **business glossary**
- A **domain model** (e.g., DDD bounded contexts)

Data contracts enforced between producing and consuming systems

A semantic layer or metric store for analytical interpretation. The goal is not uniform storage, but uniform meaning.

Why This Pattern Matters

Without Shared Semantics	**With Shared Semantics**
"Customer" differs by system, team, and interpretation	Entities retain their core meaning across platforms
Integrations require manual reconciliation and custom logic	Data products interoperate naturally through shared standards

Business logic is duplicated in pipelines	Definitions live in one place and propagate consistently
Analytics teams re-derive metrics repeatedly	Metrics are versioned, governed, and reusable

Example: A logistics company might use PostgreSQL for transactional orders, Elasticsearch for delivery address search, and Neo4j to model route relationships. Without shared semantics, each system slowly evolves its own version of "Shipment," leading to conflicting interpretations and constant reconciliation work. By defining Shipment once at the semantic layer—clarifying identifiers, status definitions, and relationships—each system can store or index the data in the format best suited to its purpose while still maintaining a single source of meaning. Storage may differ; the concept remains consistent.

Design Considerations

- Identify the canonical entities that require strong semantic continuity.
- Maintain shared definitions in a schema registry + business glossary.
- Ensure every storage/processing pipeline maps back to this shared model.
- Evolve meaning intentionally by versioning entities and metrics.
- Apply this layer not just in design docs but in code, schemas, and catalogs.

Common Pitfalls

- Treating polyglot persistence as a "free-for-all" allowing each service to redefine business terms.
- Relying on implicit assumptions or tribal knowledge.
- Letting pipelines silently reinterpret fields (e.g., revenue → net vs gross).
- Focusing on format alignment (JSON/SQL/CSV) instead of semantic alignment.

Design Principle: Embrace storage diversity, but unify meaning. The system succeeds not because every database is the same, but because every representation speaks the same language.

Polyglot persistence is not about technology choice. It is about semantic stewardship. If meaning remains stable while storage adapts, the system scales without losing itself.

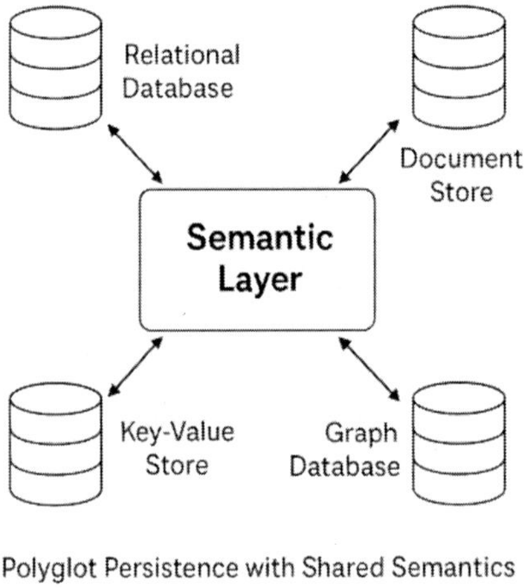

Figure 8.2 Polyglot persistence with a shared semantic layer.

Architecting the Semantic Foundation of a Data Platform

"Most data platforms don't fail at scale. They fail at semantics."

Modern data platforms are often designed to move and process data quickly but not to preserve or communicate what the data *means*. Performance, throughput, and tooling take precedence, while clarity, ownership, and shared interpretation are left implicit or tribal. The result is familiar: dashboards don't align, machine learning models behave unpredictably, and trust erodes.

The missing ingredient is not another pipeline framework or storage engine. The missing ingredient is a semantic foundation.

Where Most Platforms Go Wrong

Too many platforms are built on technical assumptions alone. Data moves, transforms, and accumulates but its meaning fractures along the way.

Common failure patterns:

Failure Pattern	Resulting Problem
Schema ≠ Semantics: Fields are defined structurally but not conceptually.	The same term (e.g., *active*, *closed*) means different things to different teams.
No Contract, Just Flow: Data producers push changes without accountability.	Downstream systems silently break.
Governance Added Too Late	Stewardship, lineage, and definitions must be reconstructed after the fact.

Business Logic Hidden in Pipelines	No authoritative source for how metrics or states are derived.
Tools Before Design	Infrastructure grows, but understanding does not.

These are not engineering problems. They are meaning problems.

What a Well-Designed Platform Actually Needs

A platform is successful not when it runs fast, but when it produces data people can trust.

A semantic-first data platform includes:

Layer	**Semantic Function**
Shared Glossary	Defines core business terms with agreed meaning.
Data Contracts	Align schema, semantics, and obligations between producers and consumers.
Versioned Metadata	Captures lineage, stewardship, and quality expectations over time.
Policy Enforcement	Applies access, masking, and retention consistently and automatically.
Observable Trust Signals	Surfaces freshness, validity, and usage where data is consumed.
Composable Architecture	Allows teams to build on shared logic rather than re-invent it.

This foundation is not simply technical. It is organizational.
It ensures that meaning is shared, portable, and stable.

Design Principle: Don't just integrate systems. Integrate meaning.

A data platform without semantics is just a scalable data swamp; fast, modern, and untrusted.

Patterns for Semantic Alignment

Pattern	Primary Benefit	Best For	Risk to Watch	Tech / Tools
Event-Driven	Traceability & context	Auditing, temporal & reactive workflows	Events too fine-grained or poorly named	Kafka, Pulsar, EventBridge, Debezium
CQRS	Decoupling intent from read behavior	Complex domains & evolving models	Over-engineering simple systems	Axon Framework, MediatR, custom Kafka CQRS
Data Mesh	Domain-aligned ownership	Large orgs, federated teams	Semantics diverge across domains	DataHub, Collibra, Monte Carlo, OpenMetadata
Self-Describing Data	Interoperability & automation	ML pipelines, streaming, schema evolution	Metadata incomplete or inconsistently maintained	Avro, Parquet, JSON Schema, Protobuf
Polyglot Persistence	Model & performance specialization	Heterogeneous workloads	Meaning divergence across storage types	PostgreSQL, MongoDB, Neo4j, Redis, Snowflake

CHAPTER 9

Tools That Scale Trust, Not Confusion

"A fool with a tool is still a fool."
— Grady Booch, UML co-creator

Design and architecture can be undone by poor tooling. This chapter connects tool choices to the preservation of trust, meaning, and observability.

Technology as Enabler, Not Substitute

Modern stacks teem with warehouses, transformation engines, orchestrators, catalogs, test suites, and observability layers. Tools embody a design philosophy; they cannot replace one. They won't fix semantic misalignment, fragmented ownership, or missing context. They only reinforce (or amplify) the architecture and practices you already have.

Rather than list vendors, this chapter focuses on categories that uphold data-centric principles across the lifecycle: versioning, discovery, documentation, validation, and trust. In the AI era, trust is more than accuracy; it's traceability, intent, and accountability: not just what data is used, but why it's valid, who owns it, and how its meaning persists as systems evolve.

Treat tools not as shortcuts but as force multipliers. Aligned with thoughtful architecture, they bring discipline, visibility, and scale to fragile processes. Misapplied, they automate chaos propagating inconsistencies faster and burying flawed assumptions deeper.

How Tool Categories Reinforce Data-Centric Principles

Principle	Pipelines	Metadata	Contracts	Testing
Versioning	✓	–	✓	✓
Discoverability	–	✓	✓	✓
Shared Meaning	–	✓	✓	–
Trust (Outcome)	✓	✓	✓	✓

- ✓ = strong contribution
- – = indirect or minimal contribution

Common Failure Patterns Without These Tools

Even with modern infrastructure, data systems fail not from lack of scale, but from lack of clarity and accountability. When versioning, metadata, contracts, and testing are absent or weak, predictable breakdowns occur:

1. **Silent Schema Shifts**: Fields change quietly. Pipelines still run, but dashboards and models drift without warning. Trust erodes one anomaly at a time.
2. **Metric Drift and Definition Conflict**: Teams define core metrics differently. Dashboards multiply. Meetings become debates over whose number is "right."

3. **Governance by Memory**: Lineage and meaning live in people's heads. When someone leaves, context leaves with them.
4. **Observability Without Ownership**" Alerts fire, but no one knows who is responsible for fixing the issue. Accountability diffuses across teams.
5. **Testing as Postmortem**: Data quality issues are discovered by stakeholders not systems. Root cause analysis happens after damage is done.
6. **Contracts as Hopes, Not Guarantees**: Without enforced expectations, producers make changes that break consumers, and misalignment becomes normalized.

The Pattern: Automation Without Agreement

Modern data stacks can move and transform data at massive scale. But speed without shared meaning does not create clarity, it accelerates confusion. Without semantic guardrails, pipelines simply propagate misinterpretation faster and deeper. These failure modes are not rare; they are systemic. And they persist regardless of how advanced the tooling appears.

Example: A company adopts a cloud warehouse and modern ELT tooling. Within months, hundreds of new tables appear, each with slightly different definitions of *active customer* or *monthly revenue*. Dashboards multiply; interpretations diverge. Trust declines, not because the tools failed, but because meaning was never aligned.

Now consider the same stack with:

- **Contracts** defining expectations,
- **Ownership** clarifying accountability,
- **Lineage** making transformations visible,
- **Testing** enforcing quality.

Here, tools reinforce shared understanding rather than masking fragmentation. Tools don't create clarity but when aligned with design, they scale and protect it.

We now turn to four categories of tools that operationalize trust:

1. **Versioned Data Pipelines** — Safe evolution through reproducibility and controlled change.
2. **Metadata-First Platforms** — Discovery and context embedded into the system, not documentation.
3. **Data Contracts in Practice** — Schemas as shared, enforceable agreements between producers and consumers.
4. **Continuous Testing & Observability** — Quality and reliability enforced continuously, not after failure.

Versioning gives us history. Metadata gives us meaning. Contracts give us boundaries. Observability gives us confidence.

Together, they turn data systems from *fragile* to *trustworthy*.

1. Versioned Data Pipelines

In In software engineering, version control is non-negotiable. Every change to code is tracked, reviewed, revertible, and accountable. Yet in many data environments, transformations, schemas, and even dataset definitions evolve without traceability. When logic changes silently, dashboards misalign, models drift, and trust erodes often without anyone knowing when or why.

Versioned data pipelines bring software discipline to data work. They allow teams to:

- Track how transformations and schemas evolve over time
- Reproduce past reports, experiments, and model training runs

- Coordinate changes safely across dev → staging → production
- Maintain backward compatibility or roll back when needed
- Meet auditing and regulatory expectations for traceability

Why this matters:

If you cannot see *when* meaning changed, you cannot understand *why* outcomes changed. A small shift—like redefining revenue to exclude discounts—can cascade across dashboards, forecasts, and machine learning models. Versioning makes these changes visible, intentional, and reversible.

Example: A team manages transformations in dbt, backed by Git. Each change requires a pull request, tests, documentation, and metadata updates. Tools like DataHub annotate lineage, while Delta Lake or Iceberg retain historical table versions. When the revenue logic changes, downstream models and dashboards are automatically flagged. If needed, a previous version is restored exactly, reproducibly.

Versioning reduces fear of change. It allows teams to experiment, branch, validate, and merge with confidence. This mirrors mature software practices and enables responsible agility across the data lifecycle.

Best Practices

- Version transformation logic and schema definitions in Git
- Use schema diffing and impact analysis during pull requests
- Promote pipelines via CI/CD (dev → staging → prod)
- Pair code versioning with data versioning (Delta Lake, Iceberg, LakeFS)
- Capture *intent* in version notes not just what changed, but *why*

Supporting Tools

Category	Examples
Transformation & CI/CD	dbt, Airflow + GitOps, Dagster, Spark + CI
Data Versioning	Delta Lake, Apache Iceberg, Hudi, LakeFS, Nessie
Lineage & Change Intelligence	Datafold, OpenLineage, DataHub

Design Principle: If it changes, it should be versioned.

Versioning protects meaning, enables traceability, and turns change from a risk into a capability.

2. Metadata-First Platforms

Metadata is more than "data about data." It is the connective tissue that makes complex data ecosystems understandable. As datasets multiply and pipelines scale, metadata becomes essential for maintaining coherence, accountability, and trust. Without clear metadata, even well-modeled datasets turn into black boxes, hard to find, harder to interpret, and easy to misuse.

A metadata-first platform treats context as infrastructure, not documentation. It automatically captures lineage, ownership, schema evolution, and usage and makes that context visible where work happens. In doing so, it transforms metadata from static reference material into active decision support for both humans and systems.

Modern data architectures increasingly invoke both data fabric and data mesh as blueprints for scaling trust and interoperability. While often portrayed as competing paradigms, they are in fact complementary. A data fabric focuses on the technical layer; the connective tissue of metadata, lineage, and automation that unifies data across systems. A data mesh focuses on the organizational layer, the domain-driven model that decentralizes ownership and stewardship. Together, they provide coherence: the fabric ensures interoperability; the mesh ensures accountability. When integrated, they create architectures that preserve both meaning and motion.

Why Metadata Matters

- Makes data discoverable instead of tribal
- Supports governance and compliance at scale
- Enables root-cause and impact analysis when things change
- Clarifies ownership and accountability
- Powers automation in validation, classification, and access control

Example: When Meaning Breaks Machines

At a fintech company, churn predictions suddenly shifted despite pipelines being green and contracts valid. Nothing was *broken*—a semantic assumption had changed upstream. Because metadata did not surface the change, the team could not trace *why* model behavior shifted.
This is why metadata must live with the data—not in wikis or memory.

Core Capabilities of Metadata-First Platforms

- Automated lineage extraction (Spark, Airflow, dbt, Snowflake, etc.)
- Business glossary terms linked to real columns and metrics
- Stewardship and ownership embedded in every dataset

- Usage-based impact analysis and dependency mapping
- Policy enforcement (e.g., PII classification, retention rules)
- Embedded documentation and contract awareness in tooling interfaces

Best Practices

- Treat metadata capture as part of the data product lifecycle
- Require producers to annotate meaning as they build—not afterward
- Make metadata queryable and visible at the point of consumption
- Standardize metadata schemas and naming across domains
- Use metadata to trigger alerts, contract checks, and lineage-aware deployments

Supporting Tools

Category	**Examples**
Catalog & Glossary	DataHub, OpenMetadata, Amundsen, Collibra
Lineage & Observability	Monte Carlo, Metaplane, Soda
Policy & Classification	Immuta, BigID

Metadata and AI: The Foundation of Trust at Machine Scale

In traditional analytics, metadata improves discoverability.
In AI systems, metadata is survival.

Without strong metadata:

- You cannot trace the origin of training data
- You cannot explain model decisions
- You cannot detect semantic drift in features or labels

Metadata enables:

- Model Cards (purpose, provenance, behavior)
- Feature Stores with semantic and lineage awareness
- Automated retraining triggered by schema or distribution drift
- Explainability frameworks based on transformation and lineage history

Without metadata, models are black boxes. With metadata, they become testable, governable systems.

Design Principle: Metadata is infrastructure.

Systems that treat metadata as first-class become more interpretable, governable, and resilient. Systems that treat it as documentation eventually lose meaning at scale.

3. Data Contracts in Practice

In many organizations, schema definitions live in code, tribal knowledge, or outdated documentation. Changes happen quietly. Meanings drift. Dashboards break. Data products become brittle because expectations are implicit instead of explicit.

Data contracts make those expectations explicit.

A data contract is a versioned, testable agreement between data producers and consumers. It specifies:

- **Structure** — fields, types, keys, nullability
- **Semantics** — what values mean and which are allowed
- **Operational guarantees** — freshness, delivery cadence, ownership, retention

The contract forms a shared boundary of trust, enforceable through validation and CI/CD not just goodwill or memory.

Why Data Contracts Matter

They:

- Align expectations across team boundaries
- Catch breaking changes before they reach dashboards or ML models
- Support automated testing and deployment pipelines
- Establish clear ownership and accountability
- Reduce reliance on tribal knowledge and ad-hoc interpretation

Example: An e-commerce team defines a contract for the orders dataset:

- order_id must be unique
- order_status must be one of: pending, shipped, cancelled, returned
- created_at must be in ISO-8601 format

If an engineer modifies the application and introduces a new status (e.g., in_process) without updating the contract, the CI pipeline fails.
The change does **not** deploy until the semantic agreement is updated.
Consumers are notified automatically.

Meaning stays intact.

Types of Data Contracts

Type	**What It Ensures**	**Examples**	**Enforcement**
Structural	The dataset *looks* as expected	field types, nullability, keys	Schema registry, JSON Schema, dbt tests
Semantic	The dataset *means* what we agreed	value domains, code sets, logical rules	Contract tests, Great Expectations, CI assertions
Operational	The dataset *behaves* reliably	freshness SLAs, latency, retention windows	Observability alerts, SLA monitoring, orchestrator policies

Best Practices

- Store contracts in version control, just like code
- Use contracts as gates in CI/CD for schema or logic changes
- Validate semantics, not only structure
- Evolve contracts collaboratively—meaning is shared, not dictated
- Feed contract metadata into catalogs, lineage, and observability tools
- Alert on contract breaches in user-visible channels (Slack, email, incident queues)

Supporting Tools

- **Contract definitions:** Avro, Proto, JSON Schema, GraphQL SDL
- **CI enforcement:** Data Contract CLI, Spectacles, GitHub Actions, GitLab CI
- **Testing & lineage integration:** dbt tests, Great Expectations, OpenMetadata, DataHub, Airflow / Dagster checks

Design Principle: A data contract is a boundary of trust.

It turns assumptions into shared commitments—stabilizing pipelines, clarifying ownership, and reducing ambiguity across the entire data lifecycle.

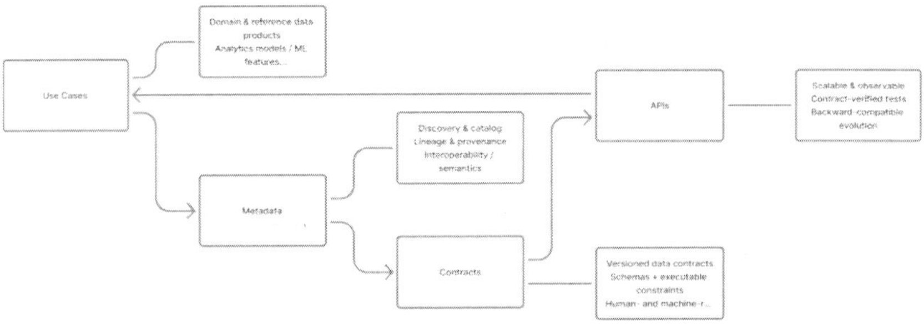

Figure 9.1 The contract-first data lifecycle. Contracts define shared meaning, APIs operationalize it, metadata makes it discoverable, and use cases close the loop with real data products and models.

4. Continuous Testing and Observability

Despite Unlike application code, data is rarely tested continuously. Many organizations still discover data issues only after a stakeholder flags a broken dashboard or a model behaves unexpectedly. Continuous Testing and Observability shift quality assurance from *after-the-fact reaction* to *real-time prevention.*

A resilient data platform validates data across the entire lifecycle:

Check Type	What It Ensures	Examples
Structural	Data conforms to expected shape	schema, keys, nullability
Content	Data values are plausible	outliers, duplicates, missing records
Business Logic	Data matches domain rules	discounts ≤ price, status transitions valid
Temporal	Data arrives on time	freshness SLAs, late-arriving partitions
Statistical	Behavior remains stable	drift detection, feature distribution shifts

Why It Matters

- Prevents bad data from reaching dashboards or ML models
- Reduces firefighting and manual troubleshooting
- Improves trust by making data quality visible and verifiable
- Supports regulated environments where traceability is required

Contract Testing vs. Data Testing

Aspect	Contract Testing	Data Testing
Purpose	Ensures schema & semantics match agreed expectations	Ensures actual data values are valid & consistent
Trigger	Runs during development / CI before deployment	Runs during ingestion & transformation
Audience	Producer ↔ Consumer boundary	Internal data & analytics teams
Failure Impact	Blocks deployment to prevent breaking dependencies	Flags quality issues before users see incorrect results

Contracts protect meaning at the boundaries; testing protects integrity in motion.

Testing Feeds Observability

Testing alone is not enough. Observability turns test results into operational signals.

Observable data systems:

- Track which datasets and domains are healthy or degrading
- Alert stewards when freshness or quality falls outside expectations
- Correlate test failures with deployment, schema, or vendor changes
- Make data health visible to both engineers and business users

Without observability, test failures are silent. Without testing, observability is only reactive. Together, they create a control tower for trust.

Supporting Tools (Examples, Not Endorsements)

- **Validation & Assertions:** Great Expectations, Soda, Deequ, Pandera
- **Pipeline Integration:** dbt tests, Dagster asset checks, Airflow data quality hooks
- **Observability & Drift:** Monte Carlo, Metaplane, WhyLabs, Datafold

Vendor & Tool Selection (Condensed Guidance)

Tools amplify your architecture; they cannot replace it. Choose tools based on semantic alignment, not just features.

Evaluate tools based on:

- Interoperability with your metadata and catalog strategy
- Support for open standards and portability
- Clarity of ownership, auditability, and governance controls
- Ability to evolve as meaning evolves

Avoiding Lock-In: Prefer systems where *your definitions, metadata, and lineage are portable* even if the vendor changes.

Security Baseline: Encryption, RBAC, audit trails, incident transparency, compliance alignment (SOC 2, ISO 27001, HIPAA/GDPR if relevant).

Design Principle: If you don't test your data, your users will.

Testing and observability transform trust from a hope into a guarantee.

Scaling Trust Beyond Foundations

With versioning, metadata, contracts, and testing in place, the question becomes how to scale trust as systems, teams, and models grow. The following capabilities expand stewardship from manual processes to continuous, automated assurance.

1. Semantic Governance with AI Agents

As data ecosystems scale, maintaining shared meaning becomes difficult—not just at the schema level, but in how metrics are defined, interpreted, and used across teams. AI agents now play a role in preserving this semantic alignment.

Semantic AI agents monitor, interpret, and intervene across the data stack not by enforcing rules rigidly, but by reasoning about meaning. When embedded in metadata platforms and observability layers, these agents act as sentinels against semantic drift.

Capabilities include:

- Detecting when a term (e.g., *"active user"*) is redefined without downstream alignment
- Flagging inconsistent metric derivations across dashboards
- Summarizing lineage and dependencies in plain language
- Suggesting contract updates when field usage patterns change
- Alerting stewards when value distributions shift or assumptions no longer hold

Example: A large e-commerce company deploys an AI agent to monitor product analytics. When return_rate suddenly increases, the agent correlates the spike with a subtle upstream change in how returns were logged and recommends both a glossary update and a strengthened contract test.

The agent doesn't replace human judgment, it scales it.

Semantic Maturity Framework for AI Systems

As AI and ML adoption increases, the cost of semantic ambiguity rises. Misaligned features or mislabeled data can produce incorrect predictions even when models are technically sound. Semantic maturity describes the progression organizations move through as they align meaning with automation.

Stage	Focus	Key Practices	Outcome
1. Syntax Compliance	Structural correctness	Schema validation, type enforcement	Reduces basic data errors in ML pipelines
2. Semantic Guardrails	Shared meaning	Data contracts, vocabularies, glossary alignment	Prevents misinterpretation and drift
3. Observable Semantics	Traceability & validation	Lineage, drift detection, contract-aware tests	Supports reproducibility and safe iteration
4. Governed Automation	Policy-driven resilience	Metadata-driven policies, anomaly alerts	Enables reliable adaptation at scale
5. Semantic Autonomy	AI-native governance	Ontology-powered agents, LLMOps	Scalable trust with minimal manual oversight

Design Insight: Semantic alignment cannot be retrofitted. It must *evolve alongside* the systems that rely on it.

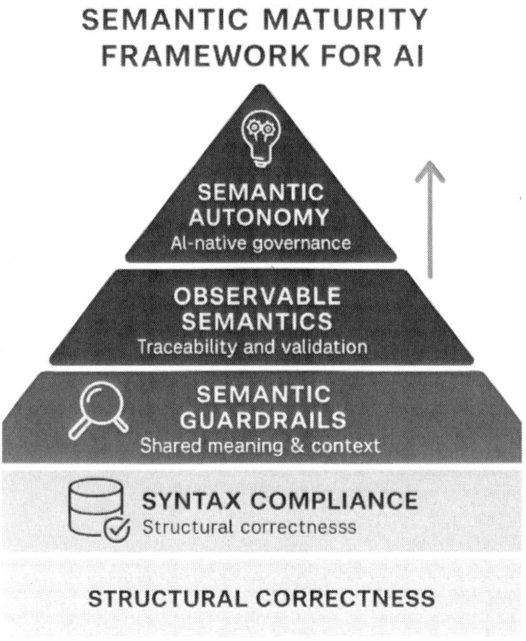

Figure 9.2 Semantic maturity framework for AI, from structural correctness to semantic autonomy.

As organizations scale semantic governance, the next step is embedding those assurances directly into the software delivery process.

6. Embedding Trust in the Development Lifecycle

In most organizations, trust checks happen too late after pipelines run or dashboards fail. Embedding semantic validation into CI/CD workflows shifts trust left, ensuring that meaning evolves intentionally and that changes to data models or contracts are deliberate, reviewed, and versioned.

CI/CD Trust Flow

1. **Trigger – Code or Schema Change**
   A developer submits a pull request introducing a schema or metric update. An automated CI job initiates semantic validation and data contract checks.

2. **Validation – Pre-Merge Tests**
   - Contract Checks: Verify schema conformity, glossary alignment, and structural integrity.
   - Semantic Diffs: Flag logic or definition drift across versions.
   - Automated Tests: Ensure referential and type consistency across dependent datasets.

3. **Review – Human-in-the-Loop**
   Reviewers receive contextual alerts for potential definition conflicts. Pull requests are paused until business and technical definitions are reconciled.

4. **Deployment – Controlled Promotion**
   Versioned tests run through development, staging, and production. Only pipelines meeting trust thresholds advance, reducing semantic drift at scale.

5. **Feedback – Continuous Assurance**
   Metrics on contract violations, glossary drift, and incident rates feed into the backlog. Governance dashboards visualize trust posture for every active data pipeline.

By embedding these checks early, organizations catch meaning and structure issues *before* production. The result is reduced rework, faster recovery, and sustained confidence in how data is defined, tested, and evolved across systems.

Example: At a healthcare analytics firm, schema changes once broke dozens of production dashboards because "provider_type" was renamed without notice.
After embedding semantic validation into their Git-based CI/CD process:

- Each pull request triggered a contract validation job.
- Violations automatically blocked merges and notified data stewards.
- Governance dashboards tracked pass/fail history over time.

Within three sprints, schema-related incidents dropped by 70 %, and downstream reconciliation work nearly disappeared.
Trust became measurable, not aspirational.

Design Principle: Treat data quality and semantic alignment as executable checks, just like unit tests.
When contracts, validations, and metadata rules are embedded in CI/CD:

- Trust becomes part of delivery, not a post-hoc audit.
- Governance becomes invisible, because it's automated.
- Change becomes safer, because meaning is versioned.

CHAPTER 10

Designing Trust: Governance and Meaning in the Age of AI

"Culture eats strategy for breakfast."
- Peter Drucker

What we build must also be governed. But effective governance isn't control, it's clarity. This chapter builds on earlier contract and architecture patterns to show how trust is embedded in roles, rituals, and guardrails.

The Broken Schema and the Blameless Pipeline

The deployment passed. Tests were green. CI/CD showed "success."

But the next morning, the marketing team's campaign scoring system failed. Leads stopped progressing. Downstream models began returning empty predictions. No one noticed for two days.

When the issue finally surfaced, no one knew who owned the problem.

The data engineer had changed the schema.
The marketing ops team had built the consuming logic.

The data warehouse had accepted the new structure without complaint. Alerts had fired but to an unmonitored channel.

A single column name had changed.
And yet an entire business workflow collapsed quietly.

When the CTO asked, *"How did this go live with no owner, no validation, and no warning?"* the answer was clear:

Because that's how things were designed to work.

The pipelines were automated, but responsibility wasn't.
Quality was tested syntactically, but not semantically.
The system had automated *movement*, not *meaning*.

Fixing the problem didn't require a new tool. It required:

- Clear ownership
- Contract enforcement
- Guardrails built into workflows

In other words: governance by design, not after-the-fact policing.

From Awareness to Action

Understanding the principles of data-centric design is not the hard part adopting them is. This chapter focuses on how organizations can practically evolve from tool-centric chaos to data-first coherence. It offers actionable guidance for leaders, architects, and teams aiming to make trust, alignment, and usability foundational to their data systems.

We'll cover:

1. **Start with Culture, Not Tools** – Lay the groundwork for long-term change.
2. **Build a Data Product Mindset** – Treat data assets like real products.
3. **Create the Right Roles** – Shift responsibility and ownership.
4. **Implement Guardrails, Not Gates** – Scale governance through automation.
5. **Measure What Matters** – Align incentives and track real progress.

Each section offers practical starting points, examples, and strategies for moving from insight to execution.

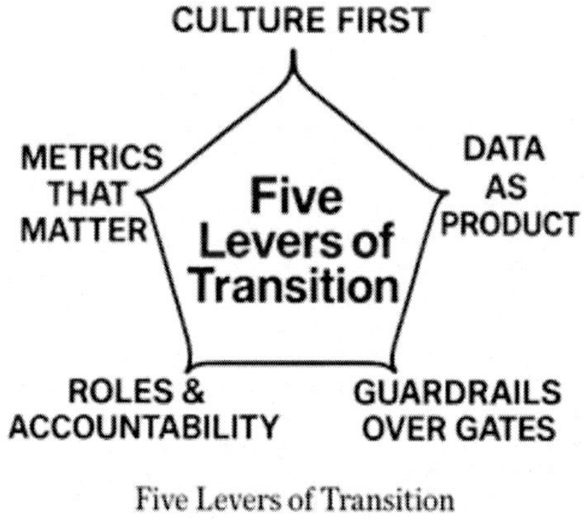

Figure 10.1 Five levers of transition: culture, metrics, roles, product thinking, and guardrails.

1. Start with Culture, Not Tools

When organizations seek to modernize their data strategy, they often begin with technology procurement: selecting a new catalog, pipeline orchestration tool, or visualization platform. But sustainable change in data maturity rarely starts with tooling. It begins with cultural transformation; the shared mindsets, behaviors, and incentives that shape how teams relate to data.

Data culture goes beyond literacy. It's about how decisions get made, how ownership is defined, how disagreements are resolved, and how quality is maintained. A strong data culture recognizes that clarity, trust, and accountability matter as much as speed and scale.

Key Cultural Foundations

- **Shared Vocabulary**: Ensure teams use consistent definitions for key terms. Align on what "customer," "engagement," or "revenue" means before debating metrics.
- **Psychological Safety**: Encourage teams to question data quality and challenge assumptions without fear of blame.
- **Embedded Ownership**: Make data stewardship part of the daily work of product, engineering, and analytics, not an isolated function.
- **Transparency by Default**: Expose lineage, freshness, and usage metrics across the organization.

Tools fail silently when meaning is unclear. Culture fails loudly when ownership is absent.

Example: Rethinking Dashboards

In one organization, every team could publish dashboards to a shared BI tool. Over time, hundreds of conflicting dashboards emerged, each claiming to be authoritative. Instead of starting with a new visualization product, leadership paused new dashboard creation and led a cross-team initiative to align on terminology, retire duplicates, and assign ownership. The result: fewer dashboards, higher trust, and faster insight delivery.

Starting Steps

- Run a data culture audit: What are your shared definitions? Who owns which datasets? What happens when something breaks?
- Host regular data roundtables: Invite teams to surface friction points and misalignments.
- Celebrate data improvements: Publicly acknowledge when teams clean up pipelines, define contracts, or improve documentation.

Design Principle: Culture sets the conditions in which good tools can thrive. If your team doesn't share meaning or ownership, no platform will fix it.

2. Build a Data Product Mindset

Traditional data teams often treat datasets as outputs, side effects of applications or pipelines. But in a data-first organization, data is a product: it serves customers, has quality standards, and evolves over time. Adopting a data product mindset means managing data with the same rigor and care applied to software or physical products.

What Is a Data Product?

A data product can be a dataset, API, dashboard, or model that is:

- **Purposeful**: It solves a specific business problem or supports a known use case.
- **Discoverable**: Others can find and understand it without deep tribal knowledge.
- **Reliable**: It's monitored, versioned, and validated regularly.
- **Owned**: A team is accountable for its freshness, quality, and evolution.

- **Documented**: It includes metadata, usage guidance, and known limitations.
- **Usable**: It has clear interfaces and is accessible with minimal friction.

Mindset Shift

From (Old Mindset)	To (New Mindset)
Shipping tables to downstream systems with unclear lineage	Designing data products with users in mind
Responding reactively to broken reports or failed jobs	Tracking usage, feedback, and user satisfaction
Assuming IT or data engineers are solely responsible for quality	Evolving schemas intentionally and transparently
Delivering outputs without measuring business impact	Thinking in terms of customer journeys and lifecycle management

Example: Revenue Metrics as a Product

A finance team redefined their core revenue table not as a raw dump, but as a governed product. They created a versioned dbt model with tests, ownership metadata, and changelogs. Every consumer—finance analysts, product teams, and executive dashboards—was informed of changes via release notes. This reduced confusion and built trust across the company.

Practices to Adopt

- Create templates for data product onboarding: define fields, owners, tests, SLAs, glossary links, and release cycles.

- Use metadata platforms to surface discoverability, usage frequency, and data lineage.
- Treat schema changes as product releases: version, communicate, deprecate responsibly, and track breaking changes.
- Monitor adoption and quality as part of the product lifecycle.
- Establish product reviews: conduct retrospectives to assess adoption, quality, and support load.

Organizational Enablers

- Assign data product managers to curate roadmap, feedback, and cross-team dependencies.
- Align incentives: reward teams for quality, adoption, and reusability not just volume of output.
- Connect data strategy to user outcomes: clarify how each product supports analytics, decision-making, or AI.

"A data product without a feedback loop is just a dataset."

Design Principle: If you want people to trust and reuse data, treat it like something worth maintaining. A data product mindset turns technical assets into durable, useful solutions that evolve with business needs.

3. Create the Right Roles

Many data problems are not technical, they are organizational. A well-architected platform can still fail if no one owns the data, if definitions aren't governed, or if quality is everyone's job but no one's responsibility. Creating the right roles and giving them authority, accountability, and support is a critical step in becoming truly data-first. Without clear responsibilities, teams default to assumptions, resulting in fragmentation, duplication, and mistrust.

Key Roles to Establish

- **Data Product Owner**: Defines and manages the vision, quality standards, roadmap, and evolution of a data product. Partners with stakeholders to prioritize features, align with downstream needs, and communicate changes.
- **Data Steward**: Acts as the semantic guardian. Ensures consistent definitions, resolves conflicts, and enforces business rules. Stewards don't own pipelines, they own meaning.
- **Domain Data Lead**: The technical architect for a domain's data flow. Designs transformations, ensures reliability, manages contracts and schema evolution.
- **Data Reliability Engineer**: Monitors pipelines for anomalies, breaks, and regressions. Owns the observability layer: data quality alerts, SLA tracking, and root cause analysis.
- **Data Governance Facilitator**: Connects domains to policy. Enables shared glossaries, compliance checks, and federated alignment not as a gatekeeper, but as a guide.

At one mid-size startup, the same person wore five hats: pipeline builder, data product owner, ad hoc analyst, glossary maintainer, and contract reviewer. Burnout was high. Data quality was low. When they formalized three part-time roles instead, delivery stabilized. Ownership became clearer, and incident response times improved dramatically.

Example: Federated Ownership in Practice

At a global e-commerce company, the analytics team struggled with inconsistent revenue definitions across marketing, finance, and operations. They reorganized around domains assigning a data product owner to each and created a centralized glossary stewarded by a cross-functional council. They also introduced a reliability engineer role to reduce surprise incidents and ensure that data products had clear uptime expectations. This improved consistency, accelerated insight delivery, and clarified escalation paths.

Practices to Support Role Clarity

- Publish a RACI matrix (Responsible, Accountable, Consulted, Informed) for key data assets.
- Create onboarding guides for each role outlining tools, processes, and expected behaviors.
- Encourage partnerships between roles: e.g., product owners and stewards co-owning metric quality.
- Make role expectations visible across the organization: include in documentation, training, and internal wikis.
- Incorporate stewardship and reliability into performance reviews.
- Embed data roles into agile rituals: assign stewards to sprints, reliability engineers to incident reviews.

Design Principle: Data systems reflect the structure of the teams that build them. If no one owns meaning, lineage, or quality, it's not a technical failure—it's an organizational one. Investing in the right roles turns abstract accountability into practical alignment.

4. Implement Guardrails, Not Gates

As organizations adopt data-centric principles, a key challenge arises: how to enforce standards without creating bottlenecks. Traditional governance models rely on central approval—often slowing teams down and creating friction. But real scalability requires guardrails, not gates: mechanisms that guide good behavior automatically without blocking progress.

Guardrails are lightweight, embedded checks that prevent common failure modes while preserving team autonomy. They encode best practices directly into platforms, workflows, and CI/CD pipelines, reducing the need for manual reviews or heavyweight controls.

Examples of Guardrails

- **Schema Validation on Pull Requests**: Block deployments that introduce breaking changes without a contract update.
- **Automated Freshness Alerts**: Notify owners when a dataset hasn't updated within its SLA.
- **Column-Level Lineage and Usage Stats**: Help users avoid deprecated fields by surfacing access patterns and dependencies.
- **Access Patterns & Masking Policies**: Automatically restrict access to sensitive columns based on metadata classification.
- **Test Coverage Requirements**: Require data products to pass quality tests before deployment.
- **CI/CD Enforcement**: Use pre-merge checks to validate schema diffs, owner fields, and contract compliance.

Why Guardrails Work

- They **shift governance left**, integrating standards into development and deployment pipelines.
- They **reinforce norms consistently**, avoiding reliance on institutional memory or tribal knowledge.
- They **scale linearly** with the organization: new teams adopt policies by default.
- They **build trust**, by preventing silent failures and increasing transparency.
- They **enable autonomy with accountability**, freeing teams to move faster within safe boundaries.

Example: Scalable Data Validation

A healthcare analytics firm introduced automated guardrails for all new dbt models. Contracts were enforced through Git pre-merge checks. Each pipeline was required to define owner metadata, freshness SLAs, and basic validation tests. This system caught schema changes and ownership gaps before they reached production without a central team reviewing every line of SQL. Over time, these checks expanded to include anomaly detection, documentation completeness, and broken lineage alerts; all surfaced via Slack and centralized dashboards.

Getting Started

- Identify the most common causes of downstream breakage (e.g., nulls in critical columns, schema drift).
- Choose one place to automate a rule (e.g., test coverage check in CI).
- Make the check visible and educative—log it, report it, alert with suggestions.
- Expand coverage iteratively: from high-value datasets to all certified products.
- Align guardrails with your maturity: early teams may need simpler checks, advanced domains can enforce stricter standards.

Common Pitfalls

- Over-enforcement: Guardrails should guide, not block experimentation.
- Lack of feedback loops: If checks fail silently or remain invisible to teams, they won't drive improvement.
- One-size-fits-all policies: Tailor guardrails to domain complexity and data sensitivity.

- A silent guardrail is no better than a missing one. Governance must be visible to be effective.

Design Principle: Effective governance scales through automation. Guardrails build confidence by preventing harm—not by restricting creativity. When done well, they make good practices the path of least resistance.

5. Measure What Matters

The final and often overlooked step in transitioning to a data-first organization is measurement. Without metrics, data maturity initiatives risk becoming performative focused on visible outputs rather than real impact. Measurement provides the feedback loop that ensures data strategy stays grounded in outcomes, not activity. Trust is not just the absence of errors. It's the confidence to use data without second guessing it.

But traditional KPIs like the number of dashboards or volume of data ingested can be misleading. What matters more is whether teams trust the data, whether decisions improve, and whether the organization reduces friction over time.

What to Measure

- **Adoption**: Are data products being used? By how many teams? For how many use cases? Are certified datasets replacing ad hoc queries?
- **Trust**: How often are quality issues reported? Are SLA breaches declining? Are teams self-reporting anomalies, or discovering them downstream?
- **Clarity**: How frequently are definitions challenged or updated? Is glossary usage growing? Are metric conflicts declining across teams?

- **Ownership**: Are metadata fields like "owner" and "steward" consistently populated and maintained? Are data issues resolved faster when ownership is clear?
- **Latency and Freshness**: Do datasets arrive on time and meet expectations? Are freshness alerts trending down?
- **Rework and Duplication**: Are similar queries and dashboards being built repeatedly? Are reports being consolidated over time?
- **Data Health Signals**: Are test pass rates improving? Are anomalies detected earlier in the pipeline?

Example: Metrics-Driven Transformation

A logistics company implemented a dashboard tracking key metrics: adoption of certified datasets, percentage of data products with validated contracts, SLA compliance, and number of unresolved quality alerts. Over 12 months, contract coverage grew from 20% to 85%, SLA breaches declined by 50%, and internal survey data showed a 40% improvement in stakeholder trust. Teams began referencing certified data by default, and the number of duplicate dashboards dropped by half.

Dimension	Bad Signal	Good Signal
Adoption	Ad hoc queries dominate	Certified sets reused
Trust	Backchannel fixes	Proactive anomaly alerts
Clarity	Conflicting metrics in dashboards	Glossary usage grows
Ownership	Unassigned errors	Escalations resolved quickly

Practices for Meaningful Measurement

- Define metrics early and revisit them regularly—align them with business outcomes, not just platform usage.
- Use surveys and feedback forms to track subjective trust, satisfaction, and usability.
- Automate tracking wherever possible (e.g., CI/CD events, metadata scans, freshness logs).
- Visualize metrics in a central dashboard accessible to data producers and consumers.
- Publicize progress through newsletters, Slack updates, or town halls to maintain momentum and recognize team contributions.
- Embed KPIs into team OKRs or departmental scorecards to sustain alignment.

Pitfalls to Avoid

- **Vanity metrics**: Don't measure activity if it doesn't lead to improvement.
- **Overhead without insight**: Avoid manual KPIs that become burdensome to collect.
- **Misaligned incentives**: Don't reward volume such as the number of dashboards over value, such as trusted insights.
- **Inconsistent definitions**: Measurement itself must be governed—metrics like "adoption" or "trust" should have clear definitions.

"Don't just measure volume, measure confidence."

Design Principle: What gets measured gets improved but only if the metrics reflect real outcomes. Measuring trust, adoption, and alignment ensures that your data strategy remains human-centered and results-oriented. Metrics don't just prove progress, they shape it.

At a regional health network, a small analytics team used these five levers over 18 months. They began by aligning on patient definitions, then restructured around domain data leads and introduced guardrails for all metrics published to the clinical dashboard. By the end of the initiative, ER wait-time forecasts improved by 40%, and physician satisfaction scores doubled for analytics usability.

Data Quality Measurement & Improvement Frameworks

Effective data governance is inseparable from systematic data quality measurement and continuous improvement. Without explicit and frameworks and clear metrics, data quality often remains an abstract goal rather than a measurable, achievable standard. Implementing proven data quality frameworks allows organizations to proactively identify, track, and rectify quality issues before they escalate into operational or strategic problems.

Dimensions of Data Quality

Successful data governance starts with clearly defining the critical dimensions of data quality. These typically include:

- **Accuracy:** Data reflects the true state of the world without errors.
- **Completeness:** Data sets have no missing or incomplete records.
- **Consistency:** Data definitions, formats, and structures remain uniform across systems.
- **Timeliness:** Data is available when required and reflects the current situation.
- **Uniqueness:** Data is free from duplication and redundancy.
- **Validity:** Data complies with business rules, contracts, and semantic standards.

Frameworks for Measurement

Several frameworks can guide organizations in systematically addressing data quality:

- **DAMA DMBOK** (Data Management Body of Knowledge): Offers comprehensive guidelines covering data governance, data quality assessment, and improvement methodologies.
- **TDQM** (Total Data Quality Management): A structured approach emphasizing continuous quality improvement through clear metrics and feedback loops.
- **Six Sigma** for Data Quality: Adapts Six Sigma methodologies such as DMAIC (Define, Measure, Analyze, Improve, Control), to systematically reduce data defects.

Practical Steps for Implementing Data Quality Frameworks

1. Define Quality Standards: Clearly articulate quality requirements for critical data assets aligned to business priorities.
2. Establish Measurement Processes: Implement metrics and regular assessments across the identified data quality dimensions.
3. Automate Quality Checks: Leverage data quality tools integrated into pipelines (CI/CD processes, data ingestion frameworks) to monitor and enforce quality standards.
4. Visualize Quality Metrics: Provide dashboards to track data quality status transparently, highlighting areas needing immediate attention.
5. Continuous Feedback and Improvement: Create formal loops to incorporate feedback from data users, driving iterative quality enhancements.

Example: Data Quality Framework in Action

An insurance provider facing recurring data discrepancies implemented a TDQM-inspired framework. They identified accuracy, completeness, and timeliness as core quality dimensions. By defining clear metrics, automating regular data checks, and visually tracking progress through dashboards, they achieved:

- 25% reduction in data errors within six months.
- 40% faster reporting cycles due to fewer manual corrections.
- Improved regulatory compliance and customer satisfaction through higher data reliability.

Guiding Principles for Data Quality Improvement

- Proactivity: Prioritize early detection and prevention of data issues.
- Measurability: Always translate quality objectives into clear, quantifiable metrics.
- Transparency: Ensure quality metrics and status are openly accessible, encouraging accountability.
- Continuous Improvement: Embed iterative quality enhancement processes into routine governance practices.

Incorporating structured data quality measurement and improvement frameworks ensures your governance strategy remains proactive, measurable, and aligned with broader business objectives transforming data quality from an abstract ideal into a practical reality.

Capstone Case: Durable Trust in Logistics

A national logistics firm had long struggled with conflicting metrics, reactive firefighting, and a fractured reporting landscape. Each region operated its own stack. Analysts spent more time reconciling numbers than advising the business. A 2021 internal audit found 67 dashboards labeled "Active Shipments" each with different logic, owners, and trust levels. Leadership's first instinct was to consolidate tools.

But a technology swap wasn't enough. Instead, they launched a transformation initiative anchored around five principles:

- **Culture First**: They began with a data culture audit mapping friction points, trust breakdowns, and glossary gaps. Data roundtables exposed how often teams worked around each other, not with each other.
- **Data as Product**: Key domains nominated data product owners. "Active Shipments" became a governed, versioned dbt model with clear documentation, test coverage, and usage tracking. Consumers now referenced the same source across finance, ops, and customer support.
- **Roles with Responsibility**: The company staffed new roles including domain stewards and reliability engineers to shift accountability closer to where data was generated and consumed. Ownership was embedded into agile ceremonies and tracked in metadata.
- **Guardrails over Gates**: Schema changes and freshness SLAs were enforced through pre-merge checks and lineage-aware impact analysis. Engineers could move fast without worrying about silent breaks or policy bottlenecks.
- **Metrics that Matter**: Progress was tracked via a centralized dashboard showing contract coverage, glossary adoption, incident response time, and stakeholder satisfaction. Within a year, certified data reuse increased 3x. Data escalations dropped 60%. For the first time, business leaders began referring to analytics as a 'core asset,' not a liability.

The turning point wasn't a tool or a migration milestone. It was when teams stopped saying "my dashboard" and started asking "is this the right product to trust?"

As organizations introduce AI and ML systems, the same governance principles must now apply not just to people but to the models themselves. The challenge is no longer only documenting meaning for humans, but encoding it so machines can interpret and act on it consistently.

Semantic Governance in the Age of AI

The adoption of machine learning systems and large language models (LLMs) introduces new failure modes that traditional data governance doesn't fully address. As organizations scale AI capabilities, they must grapple with data drift, feature ambiguity, and black-box behaviors that erode trust.

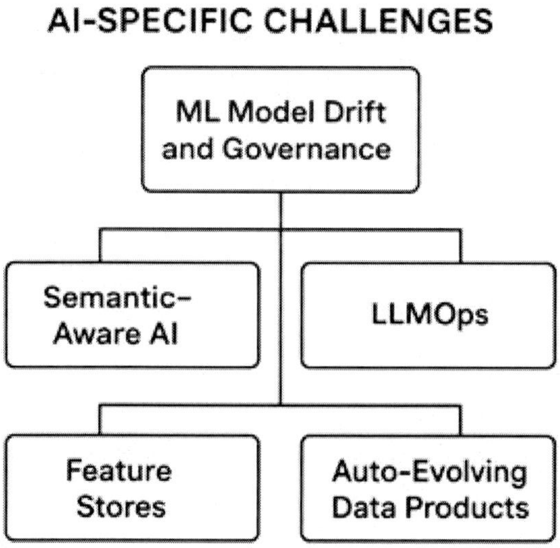

Figure 10.2 AI-specific challenges: drift, semantic-aware AI, LLMOps, feature stores, and auto-evolving data products.

Semantic-Aware AI

Semantic-aware AI refers to models and pipelines that integrate metadata, domain meaning, and semantic constraints into their training and inference cycles. This includes:

- Embedding semantic contracts into training data pipelines.
- Using ontologies to guide feature generation and label alignment.
- Ensuring that downstream models validate assumptions, not just inputs.

For example, if an AI system for hospital readmission prediction assumes "visit" means an inpatient admission, a semantic contract should define and enforce this explicitly. Otherwise, outpatient follow-ups might corrupt training data.

Feature Stores: The Trust Interface for ML

Feature stores are centralized repositories that manage, version, and serve machine learning features. When treated as a semantic interface, they enable:

- Consistent feature definitions across models.
- Version control and lineage tracking for features.
- Governance enforcement through access controls and metadata.

In practice, a feature like avg_claims_last_90d should include:

- Business definition.
- Transformation logic.
- Validity period.
- Responsible owner.

With this, stakeholders can trace how features impact models and detect when semantic drift begins.

LLMOps: Lifecycle Management for Language Models

Just as MLOps matured to handle conventional models, LLMOps brings operational discipline to large language models. It includes:

- Prompt versioning and testing.
- Feedback loops for alignment.
- Semantic grounding of generated outputs.
- Governance metadata to trace source context.

Semantic alignment becomes essential in tasks like summarization, classification, or policy extraction. LLMs should be guided by structured ontologies or domain-specific vocabularies to avoid hallucination and ensure relevance.

Auto-Evolving Data Products

AI systems increasingly require data products that adapt automatically:

- Schema-aware ingestion that adjusts to upstream changes.
- Self-updating documentation and semantic contracts.
- Continuous monitoring for semantic drift, not just performance degradation.

These systems often incorporate agents that monitor feature distributions, test business logic assertions, and retrain models when thresholds are breached. Semantic drift is no longer a hidden risk it becomes observable, explainable, and addressable.

Extending Governance to AI and LLM Systems

The governance of AI systems demands not just policy, but design interventions:

- **Semantic Policy Engines** that encode business rules into pipelines.
- **Explainability Layers** tied to business meaning, not just model math.
- **Federated Ontologies** enabling reuse of controlled vocabularies across domains.

When AI systems act on data, the cost of ambiguity compounds. Data governance must now include model metadata, prompt documentation, and retraining protocols.

These additions move governance from being retrospective and document-heavy to real-time, embedded, and resilient scalable to AI systems that evolve faster than traditional workflows.

Looking Ahead: Governance for LLM-Driven Systems

As generative and language-based AI models become embedded across analytics and operations, new governance frontiers emerge. Meaning drift in model outputs, synthetic-data validation, and prompt lineage tracking now join data-quality and access control as core responsibilities. Future semantic governance will need to audit not only datasets but also how models reinterpret definitions over time, ensuring that automated reasoning remains anchored to business truth.

Flow of Semantic Metadata Through an AI/ML Pipeline

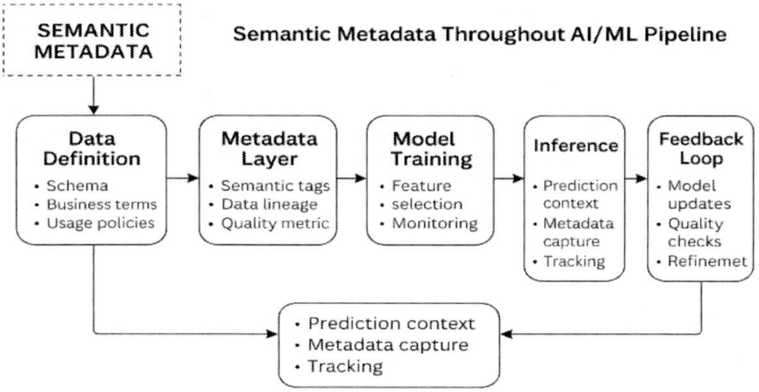

Figure 10.3 Semantic metadata threaded through every stage of the AI/ML pipeline, from data definition to feedback loops.

RDF and OWL for Semantic Governance

As data governance evolves toward machine understanding, the challenge is no longer just documenting meaning. It's encoding meaning so machines can reason with it. The shift from human-readable descriptions to machine-executable semantics allows AI systems to interpret, validate, and act upon data with contextual awareness.

At the foundation of this evolution lies the Resource Description Framework (RDF), a model that expresses knowledge as simple triples: *subject – predicate – object*. This structure allows systems to represent facts such as *"Provider → hasSpecialty → Cardiology"* in a consistent, interoperable form across platforms and databases. RDF provides the connective tissue through which disparate datasets share meaning without rigid coupling.

Building upon this foundation, the Web Ontology Language (OWL) adds a layer of logical expressiveness. With OWL, organizations can define taxonomies, class hierarchies, constraints, and inference rules that describe not just what entities are, but how they relate and behave. For instance, a governance engine can infer that if *Cardiologist* is a subclass of *Physician*, then every cardiologist automatically inherits the permissions and compliance policies applied to physicians.

Together, RDF and OWL form the semantic substrate of machine-scale trust. They transform governance from static documentation into an active reasoning system, where definitions, relationships, and policies are not merely recorded but interpreted and enforced by AI agents.

Far from being academic constructs, these standards underpin operational systems across healthcare, finance, and government from FHIR-based medical knowledge graphs to regulatory compliance engines. In modern data ecosystems, RDF and OWL integrate with metadata catalogs, data contracts, and AI governance frameworks, enabling continuous reasoning about lineage, compliance, and intent.

As AI governance matures, these semantic web standards will increasingly define how trust is computed ensuring that humans and machines operate from a shared, explicit understanding of meaning.

CHAPTER 11

From Resistance to Resonance

"People don't resist change. They resist being changed."
— Peter Senge

Tools don't change culture. People do.

And people don't resist new systems. They resist new systems with no story.

A healthcare company spent $5M on a modern stack; Snowflake, dbt, Looker. Architecture solid. Pipelines green. On paper, done.

Six months later, adoption flatlined.

Analysts slipped back to spreadsheets. Product rebuilt dashboards in silos. Executives insisted on emailed decks. They didn't trust the new ones.

Nothing was broken. Nothing was believed. Definitions weren't shared. Sources weren't trusted. No one knew why the change mattered to their work. There was a migration, not a transformation.

The lesson: change sticks when people feel the pain of the status quo and believe the future will be better for them, not just the system.

Why Change Fails Without a Narrative

Even with the right architecture, tools, and strategy, transformation stalls when there's no compelling reason to act. Data leaders often struggle not with technology, but with alignment: getting stakeholders to understand, support, and prioritize data work as a long-term investment.

The good news is that resistance isn't random, it follows patterns. When you know how to translate technical ambition into human motivation, alignment accelerates.

We'll cover six strategies that move teams from hesitation to momentum.

Expose the Cost of Inaction

Data initiatives often stall because the pain of the current state isn't visible. Stakeholders may believe things are "good enough," unaware of the hidden drag caused by misalignment, rework, and ambiguity. Making the cost of the status quo explicit creates urgency.

Common Signs of Hidden Data Debt

- **Inconsistent Metrics:** Teams spend hours debating which report is "right."
- **Manual Workarounds:** Analysts constantly export and reconcile spreadsheets.
- **Slow Decisions:** Leaders delay action while they "double-check the numbers."
- **High Onboarding Effort:** New hires struggle to learn which datasets to trust.
- **Siloed Definitions:** Core terms (e.g., *customer*, *churn*) vary across teams.

How to Make the Case

- **Quantify Rework:** Measure hours spent reconciling, repairing, or explaining data.

- **Highlight Missed Opportunities:** Connect delays to revenue, customer experience, or operational impact.
- **Use Real Incidents:** One painful example is more persuasive than theoretical risk.
- **Estimate the Cost of Delay:** Show what a week of slowed decision-making actually costs.

When waste, friction, and uncertainty are made visible, change stops feeling like an upgrade and starts feeling necessary.

Economic Considerations: Data Debt and Semantic ROI

Too often, data initiatives fail to resonate with stakeholders because the economic implications remain hidden or misunderstood. Clarifying the financial cost of poor data practices—what can be termed "Data Debt"—and demonstrating the return on investment (ROI) of semantic and governance improvements can significantly strengthen the case for strategic data transformations.

The Cost of Data Debt

Data debt accrues silently when organizations neglect semantic clarity, metadata management, and governance. It manifests as wasted time, duplicated efforts, delayed decisions, and lost business opportunities. Just like technical debt in software development, data debt increases over time, quietly eroding productivity and trust until its cost becomes painfully apparent.

Consider the following representative calculation of annual data debt:

Example Calculation	**Annual Cost**
Hours spent reconciling conflicting reports (300 hours/year @ $45/hour)	$13,500
Lost revenue due to delayed product launches	$50,000
Missed opportunities from poorly targeted campaigns due to mistrusted data	$100,000
Regulatory fines or compliance costs due to governance failures	$75,000
Total Annualized Data Debt	$238,500

Clearly articulating these hidden expenses helps stakeholders understand the urgency of addressing data issues proactively.

ROI of Semantic Investments

Addressing data debt requires upfront investments in semantic infrastructure, metadata platforms, and robust governance practices. To justify these investments, organizations need a measurable ROI framework. Here's how investments in semantics and governance translate into tangible business value:

- Reduced reconciliation time: Clear, shared definitions and semantic contracts eliminate redundant reconciliation work, directly saving analyst hours.
- Accelerated decision-making: Trusted data reduces latency in decision cycles, enabling faster responses to market opportunities.

- Lower operational risks: Governance frameworks reduce regulatory risks and potential compliance fines.
- Enhanced revenue potential: Accurate segmentation, targeting, and personalization powered by clear semantics drive higher revenue from marketing and sales efforts.

Consider a scenario: A mid-sized enterprise invested $150,000 in semantic governance (tools, training, and personnel). Within the first year, they realized:

Benefits Realized	Annual Value
Reduction in analyst reconciliation hours (200 hours/year @ $45/hour)	$9,000
Accelerated decision-making reducing product launch delays by 20%	$20,000
Reduced regulatory risk and fines	$40,000
Increased revenue through better-targeted campaigns	$80,000
Total Annualized Benefits	$149,000
Initial Investment	($150,000)
Payback Period	~12 months

After the initial year, the continued annual benefits far exceeded the recurring maintenance cost, making the semantic investment a clear financial win.

Framing Economic Conversations

When discussing economic considerations:

- Quantify costs: Always translate abstract issues into clear, financial terms.
- Highlight urgency: Use real examples of lost opportunities or tangible costs incurred due to poor data practices.
- Demonstrate quick wins: Start small, demonstrate measurable results quickly, and expand based on clear ROI evidence.

Incorporating these economic considerations into your narrative ensures that data transformation initiatives resonate strongly, securing sustained support from stakeholders who understand both the cost of inaction and the tangible returns on data investments.

Frame the Opportunity – Show What Good Looks Like

Once the cost of the current state is clear, the next step is to paint a compelling vision of the future. Stakeholders are more likely to support change if they can see what success looks like and how it solves their real-world problems.

Framing the opportunity means articulating a concrete, relatable outcome. Not just 'trusted insights,' but what it enables: faster launches, better forecasts, simpler compliance, empowered teams. It transforms data from an IT concern into a business enabler.

Characteristics of a Strong Opportunity Vision

- **Specific**: Tie the opportunity to known pain points (e.g., reducing dashboard backlog, improving SLA adherence).
- **Measurable**: Use KPIs and benchmarks from successful peers or past internal efforts.

- **Human-Centered**: Describe how roles and workflows improve, not just systems.
- **Aligned**: Show how it supports strategic initiatives already underway.

Techniques for Framing the Opportunity

- **Create before/after stories:** Contrast current vs. future experiences for key personas.
- **Visualize impact:** Use diagrams, dashboards, or data flow maps to show simplification or acceleration.
- **Reference peers:** Cite case studies or industry benchmarks to ground the vision in credibility.
- **Link to growth:** Show how data improvement unlocks new capabilities: personalization, segmentation, experimentation.

Examples of Framed Opportunity

- "Instead of analysts spending 30% of their time cleaning spreadsheets, they can focus on modeling customer behavior."
- "With centralized definitions, finance and operations can finally align on what 'active customer' means reducing month-end reconciliation time."
- "Trusted insights quality will reduce rework in our machine learning workflows by 40%."

Two-Panel Vision: From Today's Experience to Future State

Today's Experience	Future State
Analysts spend hours cleaning spreadsheets and reconciling conflicting reports.	Analysts access certified metrics with clear lineage and definitions in minutes.
Product teams rely on stale dashboards and inconsistent KPIs.	Product teams use real-time, trusted metrics aligned across departments.
Business users avoid data tools due to lack of trust or unclear ownership.	Business users explore dashboards confidently, knowing sources and owners are reliable.
Definitions like "active user" or "churn" vary across departments, causing disputes.	Shared glossary and contracts standardize definitions across finance, product, and ops.
Onboarding new analysts takes weeks of guesswork and tribal knowledge.	New hires ramp quickly using documented, discoverable data assets and lineage tools.

Framing the opportunity is about showing possibility, not perfection. You're not promising utopia. You're making the future more tangible, desirable, and achievable.

Anchoring Data in Business Value

Framing data work in business terms is critical. Without a clear link to strategic outcomes, data investments are seen as infrastructure upgrades rather than enablers of growth, efficiency, or innovation. Executives don't fund pipelines, they fund reduced churn, faster product cycles, and risk mitigation.

Anchoring in business value means translating technical improvements into language that resonates with business priorities. It's about moving from "we improved schema consistency" to "we reduced reporting delays by 40%, enabling faster decision-making across finance."

How to Anchor Data to Business Strategy

- **Link data problems to key OKRs**

  Show how inconsistent definitions impact revenue forecasting, or how data downtime affects SLAs.

- **Map technical debt to opportunity cost**

  Quantify the delays, duplication, or lost insight caused by legacy systems or poor documentation.

- **Align with business priorities**

  Whether it's improving customer retention, speeding up go-to-market, or enhancing personalization, tie data quality and usability to those goals.

- **Frame data as leverage**

  Emphasize how trusted insights amplifies existing investments in AI, analytics, and automation.

Examples of Strategic Framing

- "Consolidating redundant customer tables allowed us to accelerate the rollout of a new churn prediction model by 3 weeks."
- "Improved lineage and contracts helped us respond to an audit in days instead of weeks reducing compliance risk."
- "Centralizing revenue definitions decreased cross-functional reporting conflicts, improving decision velocity for quarterly planning."

Supporting Tools and Techniques

- **Value Stories**

  Short case studies that illustrate cause-effect relationships between data fixes and business gains.

- **Joint Roadmaps**

  Co-created plans with business units that tie data initiatives to product, finance, or marketing outcomes.

- **Metrics Dashboards**

  Track KPIs like time-to-insight, data rework rates, or adoption of certified sources alongside business metrics.

Anchoring in business value isn't just about translating data into dollars, it's about elevating its role in driving execution. It turns data work from a support function into a multiplier of impact.

Layer	Improved Label	Subtext Example
Strategic Advantage	Growth & Retention	"Personalization, competitive edge"
Business Enablement	Governance & Discoverability	"Metadata, ownership, domain models"
Trust & Access	Trusted & Certified Data	"Access controls, validated definitions"
Clean Data	Reliable Foundations	"Schemas, lineage, and data contracts"

Figure 11.1 Business value pyramid from clean data to strategic advantage.

A shaky foundation makes growth fragile. But clean, governed, trusted data builds the kind of leverage that scales.

From Data to Drama: Make It Personal

Facts may justify change, but stories inspire it. While metrics and frameworks provide logical support, true commitment to transformation is emotional. To build a lasting case, make the data problem personal -showing how it impacts real people, not just systems.

Human storytelling creates empathy. It helps both technical and non-technical audiences understand how misaligned data affects colleagues, customers, and teams. A well-told story transforms an abstract issue into a lived experience; urgent, relatable, and solvable.

Characteristics of an Effective Story

- **Concrete**: Focus on a specific person, team, or incident—not abstract trends.
- **Relatable**: Choose examples that mirror your audience's real-world challenges.
- **Tension and Resolution**: Show the friction clearly, then point to how it could be avoided or solved.
- **True**: Real stories, even modest ones are more powerful than polished hypotheticals.

Story Example: The Cost of Semantic Drift

"Last quarter, the marketing team delayed a campaign by two weeks. Why? Because customer engagement data pulled from three sources didn't match. One definition of 'active user' excluded mobile traffic. Another excluded trial users. The team spent days reconciling reports, only to realize the definitions were inconsistent. The fix was simple, but the cost was $120K in delayed revenue and a hit to credibility."

Story Example: The Invisible Tax of Onboarding

"During onboarding, new analysts spend nearly 30% of their first three months just figuring out which tables are safe to use. They ask Slack. They guess. They choose the wrong table. Weeks later, their dashboard is pulled down not because they're inexperienced, but because our data isn't discoverable. Confidence erodes. So does productivity."

Mini-Framework: PEP — Problem, Emotion, Path Forward

Use this simple framework to shape stories that resonate and drive urgency.

Element	Guiding Question	Example
Problem → Friction	What real-world friction did poor data cause?	"Marketing delayed the launch because 'active user' didn't match across systems."
Emotion → Impact	How did it affect time, trust, or morale?	"Frustrated and embarrassed, the team reverted to Excel."
Path Forward → Resolution	What solution would have prevented this?	"A shared, versioned definition would've resolved it in minutes."

How to Find and Craft Your Story

- **Interview teams**: Ask for stories of friction, surprise, or manual rework.
- **Use direct quotes**: Let the people affected speak for themselves.

- **Pair stories with visuals**: Show a Slack thread, lineage map, or timeline to bring the issue to life.
- **Close with resolution**: Illustrate how the same issue would play out differently with a better system.

When change feels risky, stories make it safe. They build a bridge between technical vision and human stakes between belief and action.

Stories are not a supplement to the business case; they are the emotional backbone. They convert awareness into urgency and urgency into advocacy.

5. Mobilize Champions – Turn Stakeholders into Advocates

Change doesn't scale through mandates; it spreads through influence. To build momentum, you need champions, people inside the organization who believe in the data vision and can advocate for it in their own language.

Champions translate strategy into local reality. They resolve resistance, model desired behaviors, and help new practices feel natural rather than imposed. When supported intentionally, they create gravitational pull for transformation.

What Makes a Good Champion

- **Respected:** They carry credibility within their team.
- **Cross-functional:** They navigate both business and technical conversations.
- **Curious:** They push for clarity and challenge assumptions.
- **Communicative:** They share progress, surface blockers, and influence peers.

How to Mobilize Champions

- **Identify early allies:** Look for individuals already frustrated by data friction.
- **Give ownership, not tasks:** Position them as co-creators of the future state.
- **Equip them well:** Provide access to glossary tooling, lineage, documentation, and leadership backing.
- **Recognize publicly:** Celebrate contributions in demos, showcases, or retros.

Example: Embedded Advocates in Practice

At a large insurer, the data team recruited product managers and analysts as early semantic modeling champions. They contributed to the glossary, piloted data contracts, and hosted informal sessions to share what they learned. Because these individuals were trusted voices within their teams, concepts like "ownership" and "lineage" entered everyday decision-making not through policy, but through peer influence.

Champion Programs That Work

- **Data Guilds / Working Groups:** Shared forums to align practices and define standards.
- **Office Hours + Slack Channels:** Ongoing support for experimentation and troubleshooting.
- **Recognition / Badging:** Signals that advocacy is valued and visible.

Champion Personas Across Functions

Persona	Strength	How They Contribute	Voice of Impact
Analyst Champion	Close to the data	Surfaces friction, pilots glossary & lineage tools	"If I stop reconciling tables every Monday, I gain a full day of analysis."
Product Manager Champion	Bridges business & tech	Drives shared KPI definitions and metric ownership	"Our experiments failed because the metric meant different things."
Finance Champion	Protects credibility	Demands consistency in revenue, churn, and reporting	"This isn't just delay—it affects trust."

When champions align around a shared meaning, transformation becomes self-reinforcing. What started as a tooling initiative becomes a movement, carried by respected voices rather than top-down mandates.

Champions turn strategy into shared momentum, helping teams experience data not as overhead, but as clarity, confidence, and progress.

6. Build Belief Through Small Wins

Sometimes, words and roadmaps aren't enough. To drive belief, stakeholders need to see, touch, and experience what "better" feels like. Prototypes make the future tangible. They de-risk change by demonstrating what's possible at a small scale.

A strong prototype isn't a finished product, it's a glimpse of a better system that solves a real problem, reduces abstraction, and sparks momentum.

Why Prototypes Work

- **Reduce abstraction**: Turns strategy into something concrete.
- **Inspire momentum**: Generates excitement when others see what's possible.
- **Test assumptions early**: Surfaces both technical and organizational gaps.
- **Build confidence**: Makes transformation feel manageable, not monumental.

Examples of Impactful Prototypes

- A **sales dashboard** showing certified revenue by source, backed by schema contracts used to resolve reporting disputes.
- A **versioned definitions entry** for "active user" versioned and adopted by product and marketing preventing KPI conflicts.
- A **data contract** embedded in GitHub, where merges are blocked unless the schema passes validation ensuring confidence at scale.
- An **interactive lineage explorer** that helps executives understand why similar metrics diverge building trust through transparency.

How to Build a Prototype That Matters

- **Pick a visible, painful use case**

  Start with problems stakeholders already care about—revenue metrics, churn flags, or high-friction workflows.

- **Use existing tools**

  Build quickly using available tools like BI platforms, data catalogs, GitHub actions, or even enriched spreadsheets.

- **Co-create with a champion team**

  Partner with those who feel the friction. Their involvement builds relevance and accelerates adoption.

- **Share early and often**

  Visibility builds interest. Let others see the progress, ask questions, and request their own version.

Levels of Prototyping: From Tactical Wins to Strategic Maturity

Prototype Type	Description	Example
Tactical	A lightweight, fast win that solves a specific pain point. Often built using existing tools.	"Revenue by source" metric published in Looker, backed by metadata and a named owner.
Semantic	Resolves meaning conflicts across teams. Focuses on shared understanding and definition alignment.	A glossary entry for "active user" with versioning, exclusions annotated, and endorsed by product and marketing.
Governance	Shows how automation and policy can scale trust and quality. Demonstrates enforcement and traceability.	A CI/CD pipeline that enforces schema contracts, blocks untested changes, and alerts on semantic drift.

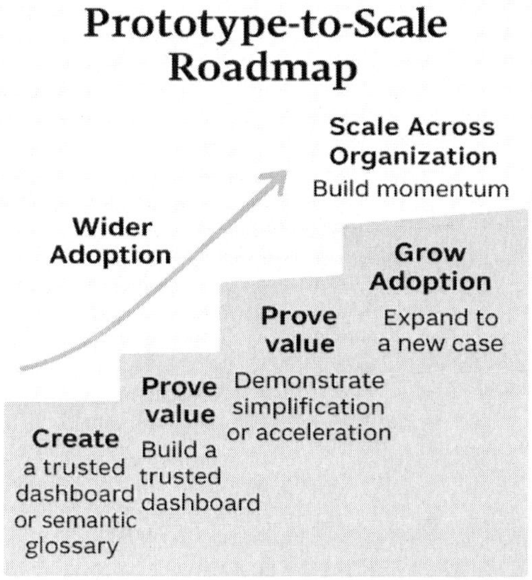

Figure 11.2 Prototype-to-scale roadmap for data products.

This roadmap shows how a small, trusted prototype can evolve into an organization-wide catalyst for trusted insights practices.

A prototype is more than a proof of concept; it's a proof of belief. It shows that transformation isn't just theoretical. It's already happening. Tangibly. Incrementally. And with the right foundation, it can scale.

You don't need to wait for funding, alignment, or perfection. A well-placed prototype can break inertia and give your data strategy its first visible win.

CHAPTER 12

From Principles to Practice

"Excellence is never an accident. It is always the result of high intention, sincere effort, and intelligent execution." — Aristotle

Now that we've covered how to design, build, and govern trustworthy systems, this chapter focuses on execution: how to translate theory into sustainable, real-world practice, even in messy, political environments

Making Data Work Where You Are

This chapter is about moving from knowing to doing turning the principles you've encountered throughout this book into consistent, practical action. Ideas alone don't shift culture or build trust. What matters is how they translate into behaviors, decisions, and design choices across the organization. Whether you're working in a nimble startup, a government agency, or a sprawling enterprise with layers of legacy systems, the first steps toward data maturity are remarkably similar. They begin not with new tools, but with clarity of meaning, ownership of responsibilities, and intentional process design.

Throughout this book, we've explored the underlying causes of failure in data initiatives. We've seen how technical problems are often downstream of organizational misalignment: conflicting definitions, unclear accountability, brittle processes, and fragmented communication. The common thread isn't bad intent. It's the absence of shared understanding and intentional coordination.

In this chapter, we focus on how to break that cycle. You'll learn five concrete strategies for translating data-first thinking into everyday workflows. These strategies are not meant to be rigid steps or best practices. They are patterns of transition: adaptable approaches that help your team make progress even when systems are messy and politics are real.

We'll walk through how to assess your current state, choose the right starting point, build local success stories, align through lightweight contracts, and embed durable practices. These are the levers of change that allow your organization to evolve, not through top-down mandates or endless migrations, but through purposeful, cumulative momentum. This chapter is both pragmatic and hopeful. It acknowledges that change is hard and shows that progress is possible. Because data doesn't become valuable when it is collected. It becomes valuable when it is understood, trusted, and used with confidence. That begins not with tools, but with design.

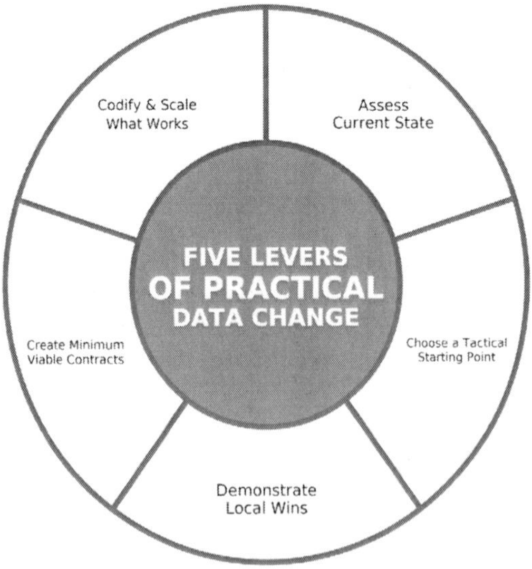

Figure 12.1 Five levers for practical data change.

1. Assess Your Current State

A candid diagnostic is the first act of leadership.

The first step in transforming how your organization works with data is to pause and look honestly at where you are. Most teams inherit mess—partial documentation, legacy pipelines, overlapping dashboards, and tribal knowledge. Change starts not by judging the past, but by making the current state visible and discussable.

This is where a data maturity assessment comes in not as a pass/fail exam, but as a structured way to uncover blind spots, establish a shared vocabulary, and focus your energy where it will have the most impact. The goal is not to be perfect; the goal is to be intentional.

Key Areas to Evaluate

To anchor the conversation, assess the following dimensions across teams and systems:

- Semantic Clarity: Do teams consistently define key terms like "customer," "revenue," or "active user"? Or do definitions vary by dashboard or department?
- Ownership and Accountability: Are data products, KPIs, and pipelines assigned clear owners? Who is responsible for fixing issues and maintaining trust?
- Discoverability and Usability: Can team members quickly find the right datasets and understand how to use them? Or do they rely on Slack threads and hallway conversations?
- Data Quality and Observability: Are there automated tests, freshness checks, lineage graphs, or quality dashboards in place?
- Cultural Alignment: Do teams treat data as a shared asset, not someone else's problem? Is there psychological safety to challenge a metric or raise a red flag?

- Delivery and Change Management: Are changes to data models, schemas, or logic tested, versioned, and communicated across stakeholders?

Sample Diagnostic Prompts

Use targeted prompts to guide conversation during workshops or interviews:

- When was the last time two teams disagreed over a metric definition? What happened?
- How many "trusted sources" exist for key entities like customers or orders?
- Can a team trace a KPI all the way back to raw source data in under an hour?
- If a pipeline breaks today, who gets notified? Who fixes it?
- When a new analyst joins, how long before they know which data sources are safe?

These aren't checkboxes—they're conversation starters that expose hidden assumptions and points of friction.

How to Use the Assessment

- Run a workshop: Bring together cross-functional voices; data engineers, analysts, product managers, business stakeholders.
- Score each area 1–5: From "nonexistent" to "automated and embedded."
- Visualize the results: Use radar charts, heatmaps, or maturity matrices to spot gaps and prioritize actions.
- Document the gaps: Don't aim to fix everything. Identify high-risk or high-leverage areas where progress will be most visible.

- Reassess over time: Maturity is not a fixed state—it evolves as your team, tools, and goals change.

2. Choose a Tactical Starting Point

Progress scales faster than perfection.

One of the most common traps in data transformation is trying to fix everything at once. Leaders often feel pressure to "standardize everything" or launch sweeping initiatives that promise consistency, governance, and structure across the entire data landscape. But broad mandates—especially those imposed without context—tend to breed resistance rather than results.

A more effective path begins with strategic restraint: identify one or two areas where improvement is both needed and feasible. These early wins serve a dual purpose. They relieve current pain and demonstrate what "good" actually looks like. Success here builds momentum and crucially, it builds credibility.

Why a Tactical Start Works

- **It focuses energy** on solvable, visible problems instead of theoretical goals.
- **It reveals real barriers** to scale—like unclear ownership, missing metadata, or downstream misunderstandings.
- **It shifts the narrative** from frustration ("Why is data always broken?") to possibility ("Look what we fixed—and how fast.")

This approach is not about "small wins" for their own sake. It's about targeting interventions that:

- Affect real users
- Have measurable business impact

- Can be replicated or generalized later

How to Choose Your Tactical Starting Point

1. **Start where the pain is loud.** Find metrics or reports that trigger daily firefights—misalignments, rework, or stakeholder confusion.
2. **Choose a team ready to act.** Avoid mandates. Partner with teams who already feel the friction and are eager to solve it.
3. **Pick a unit of work with clear boundaries.** A single KPI, a specific dashboard, a known data feed. Avoid vague goals like "fix customer data."
4. **Make the outcome measurable.** Can you track reduced time-to-insight, fewer escalations, or improved trust in a report?
5. **Plan to reuse what you learn.** Think ahead: what playbook, pattern, or checklist might this produce for other teams?

Real Example: Tactical Glossary Win

At a product-led SaaS company, the marketing team constantly clashed with sales over the term "active user." Analysts from each team maintained different SQL logic, which led to diverging numbers and endless debate.

Instead of forming a committee, a small cross-team task force agreed on a single definition, aligned it to the business model, and implemented it in dbt and Looker. They didn't advertise the change—they just started using it. When execs noticed reports aligning better across functions, they asked, "What changed?" That became the pull signal for other glossary terms to be standardized.

This was not a governance initiative. It was a local intervention with systemic impact.

Design Principle: Start where the stakes are real but manageable.

A tactical win is not just a checkbox; it's a proof point. It answers the unspoken question: *Can we really do this here, with our systems, our politics, and our people?*

Get one "yes" then scale from there.

3. Establish Local Wins Before Global Standards

Credibility comes before consistency.

In the excitement to "fix data," well-meaning leaders often start with sweeping declarations: a centralized glossary, a canonical enterprise model, or a universal set of data quality rules. But without trust, these efforts rarely stick. Teams ignore them. Friction grows. Resistance hardens.

Why? Because standards imposed too early feel disconnected from reality. They lack grounding in real experience and arrive before anyone has seen what "good" looks like. And they arrive before any part of the organization has seen what good actually looks like.

The better path is to start locally, where real pain exists and a willing team is ready to collaborate. Local wins demonstrate what's possible. They become proof points not just that data can be improved, but that doing so creates visible, meaningful value.

To prioritize where to begin, use a scoring model that considers both the pain of current issues and the value of improvement.

Starting Point Evaluation Scorecard

Use Case / Candidate	Ownership Clarity (1–5)	Visibility/ Business Impact (1–5)	Cross-Team Alignment Need (1–5)	Downstream Impact (1–5)	Feedback Loop Speed (1–5)	Total Score
Redefine "Active User" metric	5	5	4	4	5	23
Clean up legacy sales table	2	2	3	5	2	14
Contract for API transaction feed	4	4	5	5	4	22
Freshness checks for Looker dashboard	3	3	2	3	5	16
Glossary for "Revenue Type"	5	4	4	3	4	20

Why Start Local

Starting with a small, tangible success does more than solve a problem. It lays the groundwork for sustainable transformation.

- **Creates proof points**: Seeing is believing. A working example beats a 50-page policy document.
- **Builds internal champions**: Teams that experience improvement becomes advocates. They evangelize organically.

- **Produces usable patterns**: Templates, workflows, and lessons learned can be generalized and reused.
- **Prevents change fatigue**: Small, contextual change feels manageable. Broad mandates feel like overhead.

Local wins give people something to emulate and a reason to care.

How to Cultivate a Win

Local wins don't happen by chance. They must be designed to be small, focused, and contagious.

- **Start with a motivated team**: Don't sell uphill. Begin where there's already urgency or interest.
- **Solve a real problem:** Skip abstractions. Choose something tangible a misaligned metric, a broken dashboard, a fuzzy definition.
- **Make the improvement visible**: Use before-and-after comparisons, updated lineage maps, or user feedback. Capture the full journey; what was broken, how it was fixed, and what changed as a result.
- **Enable replication**: Turn success into a template: a tested dbt model, a glossary entry format, a contract checklist. Make reuse easy.

The best local wins are intentional experiments with reusable outcomes.

Example: Bottom-Up Glossary Adoption

At a SaaS company, the growth team faced constant friction around reporting "monthly active users." Three analysts worked with a data lead to define and document the term. They published it in Looker and dbt, set clear ownership, and aligned it with contract tests. They didn't pitch it to the rest of the org; they just used it.

When other teams saw the improvement, fewer miscommunications, faster reporting; they voluntarily adopted the term. Within months, the pattern spread to finance and product. What started as a local experiment became the seed for a company-wide glossary standard, grounded in a real, usable success story.

This wasn't a rollout. It was a ripple.

Design Principle: Trust grows from success—not mandates. When standards emerge from success, they gain legitimacy. When they're imposed without proof, they get ignored.

One of the most common mistakes in data transformation is premature standardization launching a universal glossary, data model, or governance framework before anyone has experienced what "good" looks like.

Example: Bottom-Up Glossary Adoption

A SaaS growth team piloted a new metric workflow with three analysts, aligning on a single term "monthly active users." They documented it, implemented it in Looker and dbt, and ownership was clear. Adjacent teams adopted it voluntarily, and within months, the pattern scaled to finance and product.

Design Principle: Trust grows from success not mandates. Local wins earn the right to scale.

4. Create the Minimal Viable Contract (MVC)

Align semantics and accountability early without overbuilding.

A data contract is more than a schema; it's a social agreement between producers and consumers. Chasing the perfect contract on day one leads to overdesign and inertia.

The answer: start with a Minimal Viable Contract, just enough shared expectation to prevent surprise breakage.

What MVC Should Include

- **Field definitions**: Semantics, not just data types
- **Ownership**: Who maintains the data?
- **Freshness**: What's the update expectation?
- **Validation**: Required tests to publish
- **Versioning**: How are changes communicated?
- **Notifications**: Who gets alerted and how?
- **Dependencies**: Who uses this? What do they rely on?

Why Small Works

- Easier adoption
- Reveals hidden semantic differences
- Encourages iteration
- Builds behavioral habits

To help teams implement their first MVC, this section breaks down the core elements and explains why each one matters.

- Surfaces systemic fragility

Minimal Viable Contract Elements

Contract Element	Description / Why It Matters
Field Definitions	Aligns intent across teams
Ownership	Ensures accountability and stewardship

Freshness Expectations	Clarifies SLA and reliability
Validation Rules	Prevents silent errors
Versioning	Supports safe evolution
Notifications	Enables proactive awareness
Dependencies	Maps impact to consumers and systems

Example: Schema Breakage to Contract Stability

A B2B fintech team cut dashboard breakages by 70% after introducing a simple contract on their "customer" table. They tracked five fields, added freshness SLAs, and included a CI/CD notification channel. Others followed suit. Another team-built test enforcement into CI turning quality into a default behavior.

Design Principle: The smallest shared expectation beats the most sophisticated undocumented system.

5. Invest in Durable Practices, Not Just Deliverables

What survives scale isn't your tools, it's your rituals.

Too often, data projects focus on outputs: a new dashboard, a migrated warehouse, a launched pipeline. While these deliverables may check boxes and win short-term praise, they rarely change the underlying system. Tools get replaced. People move on. Dashboards decay.

What endures are embedded, reinforced, and repeatable practices. These practices become part of how your organization thinks about data, not just what it builds with it. They build institutional memory and operational resilience.

Durable practices mean data quality doesn't hinge on a hero analyst or a vigilant engineer. Instead, quality becomes a default outcome of the system itself enforced by habits, automation, and social expectations.

Legacy Systems and Migration Strategies

Most data transformations don't start from scratch; they begin with a mess.

Modernizing your data practice rarely happens on a blank canvas. Organizations inherit years sometimes decades of pipelines, definitions, spreadsheets, batch processes, and tribal knowledge. Legacy systems aren't just technical debt; they represent semantic debt: embedded assumptions, undocumented rules, and mismatched definitions that quietly shape how decisions are made.

Successful data modernization doesn't mean replacing everything at once. It means migrating meaning and trust as carefully as you migrate code and infrastructure.

Common Pitfalls in Legacy Migrations

- **Schema Shift Without Semantic Review**: Migrating tables without validating the meaning behind fields leads to silent trust erosion.
- **"Lift-and-Shift" Failures**: Copying old pipelines into new platforms without questioning definitions or owners replicates old problems in a shinier shell.
- **Over-Automation Without Governance**: Automating legacy processes that were never well-defined just accelerates confusion.

Strategies for Semantically Aligned Migration

1. **Semantic Shadowing**
    - Before deprecating a legacy table or report, run the new version in parallel.
    - Compare outputs, validate assumptions, and involve stakeholders in spotting differences in logic or interpretation.
2. **Metadata Extraction from Legacy Code**
    - Use lineage tools or lightweight audits to reverse-engineer logic from stored procedures, ETL scripts, or Excel models.
    - Document embedded business rules and convert them into semantic contracts or glossary entries.
3. **Contract-First Refactoring**
    - Use data contracts as the baseline for refactoring transformations or pipelines.
    - Define the target semantics first—then map legacy logic to the desired definitions.
4. **Staged Deprecation with Trust Metrics**
    - Don't sunset a legacy table just because the pipeline runs in dbt now.
    - Track usage, ownership, and data quality trends before decommissioning.
5. **"Don't Break the Dashboards" Rule**
    - Legacy dashboards are often the most visible—and emotionally loaded—artifacts.

- Plan transition sprints that migrate definitions behind the scenes while preserving front-end continuity.

Example: Gradual Migration, Lasting Trust

A large healthcare organization attempted to migrate its claim-processing pipelines from Informatica to dbt. Initially, they focused only on performance gains neglecting to revalidate semantic alignment. Analysts reported mismatched counts, and trust eroded. Midway through, the team pivoted: they introduced semantic review checkpoints, brought in glossary stewards, and ran old and new models side by side. The result? Increased adoption, reduced rework, and eventual decommissioning of 80% of legacy pipelines with stakeholder trust intact.

Design Principle: Migration isn't just about platform lift; it's about meaning shift.

Modernization succeeds when semantic alignment, ownership, and observability are migrated along with the code.

What Makes a Practice Durable

To build long-term resilience, a practice must be more than a checklist. It must be:

- **Documented**: Clearly written, accessible, and versioned—so others can follow it.
- **Automated**: Reinforced by tooling (e.g., CI/CD, data tests) instead of reliant on memory.
- **People-agnostic**: Able to survive turnover—ownership may shift, but the practice continues.
- **Iterative**: Includes built-in review and feedback mechanisms to adapt as systems evolve.

- **Leader-modeled**: When executives and managers follow the same rituals, others will too.

The following real-world patterns illustrate how durable practices take root in high-trust teams.

- **Embedded in delivery**: Not an afterthought integrated into how work gets done (e.g., code reviews, sprint planning, releases).

When a practice is durable, it becomes muscle memory, just how things are done.

Examples of Durable Practices

Here are patterns observed in high-maturity teams:

- A **shared process** for defining and approving new KPIs, involving both business and data owners.
- **Schema contracts and quality tests** automatically enforced in CI/CD before any model change is merged.
- **Glossary terms** linked directly within dashboards and data tools ensuring semantic alignment at the point of use.
- **Monthly or quarterly data forums** where cross-functional teams review key metrics, test results, and usage trends.
- **Metadata tracking** for ownership, certification status, and data freshness visible to end users.
- **Data reliability scorecards** shared in quarterly business reviews, tracking trends in freshness, test coverage, and usage.

These practices build confidence not only in the data—but in the teams that manage it.

Building It In

You don't need to invent these practices from scratch. You likely already have them in fragments. The goal is to capture, reinforce, and scale them.

- **Start with what works:** Find habits that build trust or quality and codify them. Codify them.
- **Turn tribal knowledge into playbooks**: Write down workflows and decisions that are working—share them.
- **Automate the repeatable**: Use CI, metadata tools, and alerts to reduce manual QA.
- **Create lightweight rituals**: Don't overengineer, start with "Friday Data Check" or "First-Monday Metric Review."

Let's pause here to consider why semantics isn't just a technical detail. It's the foundation of trustworthy data products.

- **Onboard through the process**: If a new hire can follow it within two weeks, it's real. If not, simplify.
- **Track adoption and evolution**: Report % of glossary terms reused, tests passing, contracts versioned. Treat this as a product KPI.

Think of data culture as an operating system. Deliverables are apps, practices are the kernel. They define how the system behaves under pressure, during growth, or after staff changes.

Design Principle: Treat process like infrastructure. What's easy to repeat is easy to scale and impossible to ignore.

Transformation isn't achieved through dashboards, pipelines, or new platforms. It's achieved when meaning is shared, ownership is clear, and improvement becomes routine. The organizations that succeed treat data not as exhaust, but as a product; designed, maintained, and evolved with care. Progress doesn't come from grand gestures. It comes from consistent, visible wins that build trust and shift behavior. Start small. Make meaning explicit. Create habits that outlast individuals. That is how data work becomes durable.

CHAPTER 13

Future-Proofing Your Data Practice

"The future is already here; it's just not evenly distributed."
— William Gibson

Practice must evolve. As we build for scale, AI, and regulatory shifts, this chapter explores how to make data practices adaptive, resilient, and ready for uncertainty.

Designing for the Unknown

Modern data landscapes are defined by constant change: new regulations, emerging AI technologies, cloud-native architectures, and evolving organizational needs. The systems you design today must be flexible enough to accommodate tomorrow's uncertainty.

Future-proofing is not optional; it's a design discipline. It means de-coupling meaning from tools, distributing ownership without chaos, and creating visibility without micromanagement. In short, it's the shift from reactive firefighting to adaptive design.

This chapter lays out how to prepare your organization not for one future, but for the inevitability of many. Whether scaling from startup to enterprise, expanding into regulated markets, or enabling responsible AI, the foundation remains the same: clarity, accountability, and evolvability.

All of the forces shaping the future—AI readiness, regulatory agility, and organizational scale—depend on the same foundation: shared meaning that persists across tools, teams, and time. This chapter is not about adding new capabilities, but about designing semantic integrity so that every future capability can be trusted.

The tools, platforms, and regulations of today will not be the same five years from now. But the need for trustworthy, understandable, and adaptable data will only grow. Future-proofing isn't about chasing the right stack. It's about building systems and cultures that can evolve.

Whether preparing for model interpretability, responding to shifting privacy laws, or scaling semantic consistency across dozens of teams, durable data organizations start by investing in shared clarity and accountable ownership.

Future-proofing is not a singular initiative. It's a set of capabilities. In this chapter, we explore how to:

- Design for machine learning that can withstand real-world drift.
- Treat compliance as adaptive, semantic infrastructure.
- Scale meaning across teams through stewardship and literacy.

These are not separate challenges; they are facets of the same goal: designing for adaptability.

Section 1: Experiments to Endurance: Readying for AI

Machine learning is not fragile because it's complex, it's fragile because it inherits every ambiguity and assumption from upstream. In a world increasingly run by models from fraud detection to product recommendation semantics isn't just metadata. It's infrastructure.

Modern AI systems must be interpretable, auditable, and future-ready. Accuracy alone is no longer enough. Without shared understanding, even high-performing models become brittle, biased, or opaque.

To future-proof your ML systems, you must move beyond experimentation velocity toward *governed durability*. That means:

- Embedding data contracts into ML pipelines to validate inputs before training begins.
- Tracking feature lineage from raw signal to engineered value with clear links back to source systems.
- Storing human-readable definitions for every production feature in a semantic registry, not just inside notebooks or code comments.
- Testing input integrity over time, not just model performance at deployment.

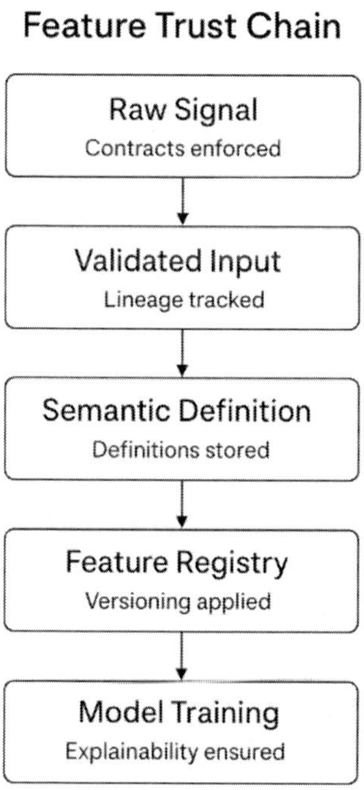

Figure 13.1 Feature trust chain from raw signals to model training.

Case Snapshot: Sensor Drift & Login Loops

A manufacturing company built a predictive maintenance model using "load" sensors, only to learn later that one plant used it to mean *torque*, while another meant *weight*. Similarly, a retail company deployed a churn model that relied heavily on a "last login" field unaware that the field was also reset during password changes. Both models appeared accurate in training but failed in production. In each case, the real issue wasn't the algorithm. It was the lack of semantic clarity upstream.

These are not isolated errors, they are symptoms of systems optimized for iteration, not integrity. Machine learning amplifies the cost of semantic misalignment. It turns tribal knowledge into institutional risk.

✓ **Checklist: To Make ML Durable**

- Use data contracts to enforce assumptions before training.
- Maintain a feature registry with lineage and business definitions.
- Version control both data inputs and semantic meaning.
- Include integrity tests in model CI/CD pipelines.
- Review feature semantics during model handoff, not just code reviews.

The future of machine learning doesn't depend on bigger models. It depends on better assumptions. And that starts with trusted definitions, verified upstream, and reinforced over time.

Section 2: Compliance as Code - Agility by Design

Compliance isn't just a legal function; it's a design discipline. And in an era of accelerating regulation, future-ready systems must treat compliance as semantic infrastructure, not brittle code. Regulations change. Business models evolve. But when governance is hardcoded into pipelines or tied to static logic, every legal update becomes a refactor. The result? Lag, cost, and risk.

Regulatory agility means building compliance that evolves as fast as your business. It starts by separating *policy logic* from *execution logic*:

- Regulations define abstract categories: e.g., personally identifiable information (PII), financial indicators, biometric data.
- The data platform maps these categories to concrete fields; semantically, not manually.
- Enforcement happens dynamically, driven by metadata, not scattered scripts.

Regulation	Key Requirement	Tooling Capability to Support
GDPR	Data access, deletion, consent	Metadata tagging, lineage, access logs
CCPA	Opt-out rights, data sales tracking	Consent tracking, audit-ready logs
HIPAA	Health info protection, audit trails	Role-based access, encryption, PHI tagging
SOX	Financial reporting accuracy	Data lineage, version control
PCI DSS	Payment data protection	Masking, encryption, usage tracking

Case Snapshot: Consent-Aware Analytics

A digital media company needed to comply with region-specific consent laws. Instead of branching code by geography, they linked data contracts to a consent_status field. Users in the EU or California triggered stricter filters, retention policies, and downstream purging, all enforced automatically. Analysts still wrote simple, universal queries. The system enforced compliance behind the scenes.

This is the power of compliance-as-code: *semantic abstraction plus execution automation*. You don't rewrite logic every time a law changes. you reconfigure a rule.

Principles of Future-Ready Compliance

1. Treat classification as metadata – "Customer ID" isn't just a column; it's a governed category with a lifecycle.
2. Link enforcement to semantics – Retention, masking, or access logic should follow the data's meaning, not just its location.
3. Enable auditability by default – Lineage, access logs, and definition history should be quarriable and versioned.
4. Design for revocation and downstream erasure. When consent is withdrawn, dependent assets must respond automatically.

Case Snapshot: Consent Triggers in Action

A fintech company integrated consent metadata into their data contracts. When users revoked consent, the system triggered downstream purges, flagged dependent models for retraining, and updated dashboards accordingly. There were no manual tickets. No after-the-fact cleanups. Just traceable, automated responsiveness.

The Four Reflexes of Agile Compliance

When you treat legal categories as living concepts—defined, tracked, and governed through metadata—you move from checklist thinking to compliance reflexes. This isn't just safer. It's faster. And in a world of ever-changing regulations, speed is survival.

Section 3: Scaling Shared Meaning.

In small teams, shared understanding is ambient. You hear the same meetings. You tap the same analysts. But as organizations scale, that ambient clarity dissolves. Definitions fragment, assumptions diverge, and "what the data means" becomes a source of conflict, not insight.

Scaling a data practice isn't just about pipelines or platforms, it's about meaning. To scale common understanding, resilient organizations invest in two things:

1. Semantic stewardship—the systems, standards, and incentives that make meaning reusable.
2. Data literacy—the cultural capacity to interpret and act on that meaning.

These are not separate domains. They reinforce each other. Tools without fluency fail. Fluency without clarity stalls. Future-proof data organizations build both.

Part A: Stewardship Systems – The Infrastructure of Meaning

Semantic stewardship turns tribal knowledge into shared infrastructure. It's how you make "revenue" mean the same thing in finance and product. How you version a metric. How you deprecate bad logic.

Example: Streaming Glossary Index

A video platform unified its marketing, finance, and content teams through a shared glossary hub. Their BI tools highlighted deprecated metrics and suggested certified replacements. Analysts weren't forced to comply; they were nudged toward clarity.

Tactics for Systemic Stewardship:

- Build a versioned glossary and ontology that link terms to owners, contracts, and lineage.
- Enable schema validation against semantic contracts—not just structure.
- Promote term reuse through templates, autocomplete, or policy nudges.
- Assign stewards within each domain, not just in a central team.

Part B: Semantic Portability

Over time, teams stop asking, "What does active user mean here?"—because the answer is embedded, governed, and visible.

Avoiding Vendor Lock-In with Semantic Abstraction

Designing for adaptability means decoupling meaning from platform. When semantic layers like glossaries, metric definitions, and data contracts are defined independently of specific BI tools or data warehouses, organizations gain resilience. This abstraction ensures that definitions of "customer," "retention," or "revenue" persist even if the underlying technology stack evolves. Whether switching from Tableau to Looker or from Snowflake to Databricks, interoperable semantic models prevent costly rework and preserve shared understanding. True data agility comes not from tool features, but from owning your language and making it portable.

Semantic Portability: Surviving Stack Swaps

Without Semantic Layer	With Semantic Layer
Metric logic embedded in dashboards	Centralized, reusable metric definitions
Migration rewrites 100+ reports	Migration updates shared layer once
Tool dictates how "customer" is defined	Business defines "customer" once, reused
High vendor dependency	Platform-agnostic governance layer

Part C: Scaling Data Literacy

Semantic infrastructure only works when people can use it. Data literacy isn't about one-time training—it's about developing role-specific fluency in how data is interpreted, discussed, and applied.

Example: Embedded Data Coaching

A retail chain embedded "data coaches" within business units—analysts who hosted office hours, translated glossary terms, and guided better metric design. Report volume decreased and trust increased. Why? Because teams didn't just consume data—they understood it.

Tactics to Scale Literacy

- Create role-specific data playbooks for PMs, marketers, finance, and operations.
- Embed data concepts into onboarding and recurring training, not one-off workshops.

- Run collaborative modeling sessions when definitions or metrics evolve.
- Include data health and trust indicators in business performance reviews.

At a logistics firm, pairing analysts with operational leads for short "data fluency sessions" didn't just improve adoption—it improved the glossary itself. Meaning became sharper through use, feedback, and shared interpretation.

International and Cross-Cultural Considerations

"Global alignment is not about enforcing sameness. It's about designing for meaningful variation."

As organizations expand across regions, semantic misalignment and governance inconsistency become increasingly common. The same KPI like "active customer" may be defined differently in the U.S., EMEA, and APAC. Local teams operate under different business models, regulatory pressures, cultural expectations, and even levels of data fluency.

The Challenge of Global Semantics

Globally distributed data teams face three persistent challenges:

1. **Semantic Fragmentation**
   - Core business terms take on different meanings across geographies or business units.
   - Example: "Customer" in the U.S. might refer to B2C end-users, while in Germany it includes resellers and partners.

2. **Regulatory Diversity**
   - Data residency laws, privacy regulations, and consent requirements vary by region.

  - Example: GDPR (EU) vs. CCPA (California) vs. LGPD (Brazil) often require divergent data handling practices.

3. **Cultural Expectations**
   - Teams may differ in how they define ownership, escalate issues, or engage in collaborative governance.
   - Example: U.S.-based teams might favor open data access with Slack-based support, while APAC teams prefer defined roles and formal escalation paths.

Strategies for Global Semantic Alignment

1. **Localized Stewardship with Federated Standards**
   - Assign glossary stewards within each region or domain.
   - Empower local teams to contribute and manage definitions while aligning with a central ontology.
   - Promote reuse of canonical terms with room for local extensions.

2. **Policy Variants and Semantic Inheritance**
   - Use metadata platforms that support policy branching: a base definition for "customer" can be inherited and adapted regionally with annotations and tags.
   - Avoid forcing a one-size-fits-all schema across all domains.

3. **Cross-Cultural Governance Design**
   - Establish governance rituals (e.g., metric reviews, lineage audits) that respect local work norms.
   - Provide translated glossaries or tooling interfaces if needed.

4. Semantic Audit Trails by Region

- Track where definitions diverge and why. Make semantic variation visible, intentional, and documented.
- This builds empathy across teams and helps central stakeholders understand local constraints.

Example: Global Glossary with Regional Extensions

A multinational logistics firm built a semantic hub with a core global glossary and localized overlays. Terms like "shipment" and "delivery" had consistent base definitions but were extended for regional variations (e.g., same-day in Japan, batch windowed in the EU). Each region had stewardship rights, and glossary differences were versioned and auditable. This structure enabled both alignment and autonomy, reducing metric conflicts by 60% across business units.

Design Principle: Don't enforce uniformity enable coherence.

Global alignment works best when local variation is intentional, documented, and governed.

Shared Meaning Is the Real Platform

The real difference between high-performing data organizations and the rest isn't tools. It's trust. And trust depends on shared meaning; defined by systems, reinforced by people.

Stewardship (System)	Literacy (People)
Glossary + Ontology Hub	Role-specific playbooks
Semantic Schema Validation	Embedded data coaches
Versioned Metrics	Collaborative modeling sessions
Steward Incentives	Business-level data reviews

Without stewardship, meaning fractures. Without literacy, it stagnates. With both, it scales.

The organizations that survive future shifts won't be the ones with the flashiest stack. They'll be the ones where teams speak the same language because they designed it, stewarded it, and taught it together.

Epilogue: From Stack to Story

You've just read a book about data but not really about tables, pipelines, or platforms. It has been a book about shared meaning, responsible design, and the human systems behind the technical ones.

Every organization says it wants to be "data-driven." But more dashboards don't create clarity. More models don't create trust. What endures is not the tool you choose; it's the language you share, the agreements you honor, and the culture you build around meaning.

When data becomes ambiguous, so does strategy.
When definitions drift, accountability drifts with them.
The most effective data organizations aren't the ones with the newest architecture. They are the ones that design conversations before they design systems.

Conversations about what "customer" really means.
Conversations about how "revenue" is calculated.
Conversations about who owns a metric, and how its truth is protected over time.

These are not technical discussions. They are cultural commitments.
They shape everything downstream from governance to growth, from AI trust to decision velocity.

In the end, data is not merely an asset.
It is a language we share or fail to share.
And everything else in the system reflects that.

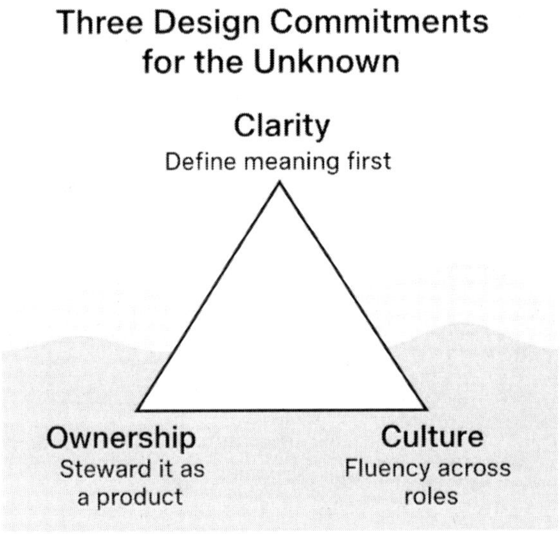

Figure 13.2 Three design commitments: clarity, ownership, and culture.

Three Design Commitments for the Unknown

In a world of constant change, resilient data organizations don't chase every trend. They make three enduring commitments:

- **Clarity over Complexity:** Define meaning before wiring systems. Make semantics visible, versioned, and governed.
- **Ownership over Bureaucracy:** Assign accountable stewards. Treat metrics, contracts, and glossaries as products; maintained, improved, and explained.
- **Culture over Tooling:** Invest in fluency across roles. Build literacy, not just lineage. Teach the organization how to think with data, not just consume it.

The future is unknowable. But the ability to adapt is designable.

Whether you're building dashboards or governing models, onboarding stewards or scaling a data mesh, your work isn't about perfection. It's about progress. About evolving toward clarity even as the landscape shifts beneath you.

Data, like language, is only powerful when it is understood. Design for understanding and the rest will follow. Future-proofing isn't just strategic; it must be actionable. The following five levers represent repeatable tactics to initiate meaningful, durable change in complex data environments:

CHAPTER 14

Meaning in the Age of AI

"Data are just summaries of thousands of stories; tell them right and they will speak truth." — Chip & Dan Heath

Finally, we examine the stakes of everything we've discussed. In the age of AI, semantic clarity is no longer a nice-to-have. It is the safeguard against misdirection, bias, and automation gone wrong.

Framing Meaning - Why It Matters Now

AI doesn't clarify truth, it amplifies belief. And if the underlying belief is flawed, so is the outcome; just faster, louder, and harder to notice. In the age of machine learning, deep learning, and large language models (LLMs), the cost of misunderstanding data has never been higher. When human interpretation is replaced or augmented by automated systems, meaning must be clear, consistent, and contractually embedded. Otherwise, the outcome isn't just error, it's confident misdirection at scale.

Today, automated systems are entrusted with decisions that shape healthcare, finance, logistics, security, and beyond. Even basic terms like *"customer"* or *"incident"* vary across departments and evolve over time, yet AI systems lack the intuition to detect such shifts unless explicitly modeled. As we delegate cognitive tasks to machines, the governance of data itself becomes a new source of systemic risk.

This chapter explores how contextual, ownership, and clarity, principles already central to data-first design, become mission-critical when AI enters the picture. From brittle feature pipelines to hallucinating chatbots, we examine where meaning breaks down and how to build systems that evolve without semantic drift.

We also introduce concepts from the broader AI and ML ecosystems such as data-centric AI, model observability, explainable AI (XAI), retrieval-augmented generation (RAG), knowledge graphs, causal inference, AI agents, and LLMOps to demonstrate how interpretive governance intersects with modern AI pipelines.

Before we look at specific failures, it's important to see what these examples represent. Each scenario illustrates a different form of semantic breakdown—proxy signals, local variation, silent drift, or inconsistent meaning across systems—and how these subtle issues quietly destabilize AI models. The details change by industry, but the pattern is the same: when meaning is assumed rather than governed, intelligent systems make confident mistakes. The following examples make that pattern visible.

Churn Model

A telecom churn model used "last login date" as a core feature. But password resets triggered logins automatically, making it an unreliable signal of engagement. The result: the model overestimated churn risk among active users, leading to unnecessary interventions.

This example illustrates the challenge of proxy signals: fields that seem intuitively aligned with behavior but are contaminated by unrelated processes. Without semantic validation, features become brittle proxies that mislead downstream predictions.

Readmission Model

A hospital system developed a readmission risk model using the field "primary diagnosis." In some departments, this recorded symptoms; in others, it held ICD-10 codes. The model failed to generalize and flagged low-risk patients, diverting resources.

Here, Local practice variation created a semantic rift invisible to statistical validation but devastating to model utility.

Credit Scoring

A regional bank's ML-driven credit scoring engine relied on a feature labeled customer_tenure, which changed definition after a CRM migration. Without relabeling, the same field now included credit accounts, inflating scores. Defaults rose by 11% in a quarter.

This is a classic case of silent semantic failure when the structure stays the same, but the meaning shifts beneath. This scenario underscores a subtle but dangerous type of drift: conceptual drift without statistical evidence. The values appeared consistent; the behavior was not.

Autonomous Supply Chains

A manufacturing firm deployed reinforcement learning agents using a field warehouse_load_factor. Some regions used numeric percentages, others used categorical labels. The reward function misinterpreted load metrics, skewing optimization and compounding errors over time.

This is an example of semantic collision where heterogeneous data formats with incompatible meanings are fed into a uniform logic. Reinforcement learning, with its recursive feedback loops, amplifies such flaws exponentially.

Problem Type	Root Cause	Model Impact
Proxy Signal Contamination	Field used for proxy is altered by unrelated systems	False positives/negatives due to noisy feature
Local Practice Variation	Field used differently across departments	Poor generalization across subgroups
Silent Semantic Drift	Field redefined without schema or label change	Undetected drop in prediction quality
Semantic Collision	Inconsistent units or formats across regions	Policy skew and compounding reinforcement errors

The pattern across these failures is not technical. It is semantic. The models did exactly what they were trained to do. The meaning of the data changed, and the systems had no way to recognize it.

Principles of Semantic Resilience

In every resilient data system, meaning must endure change.
Semantic resilience is the ability of definitions, relationships, and rules to evolve without breaking trust. It connects the tactical world of data contracts with the conceptual depth of ontologies—ensuring that as systems grow, they don't drift away from the human understanding they were built to serve.

Principle 1: Field-Level Semantic Contracts

A schema defines structure; a contract defines meaning. Schema validation alone cannot prevent semantic erosion.

Aspect	Schema	Semantic Contract
Definition	Defines structure and data types	Defines meaning, intention, and business context
Validation Level	Syntactic	Semantic
Focus	Shape and format	Purpose and use
Detection Timing	During data load or ingestion	During transformation, training, or inference
Enforced By	Validators, parsers	Business rules engine, SME-approved policies
Example Violation	Field is null or wrong data type	Field labeled 'historical' contains future date

Organizations like the aforementioned bank introduced contract-driven feature registries with SME-verified annotations, expected distributions, and flags for semantic drift.

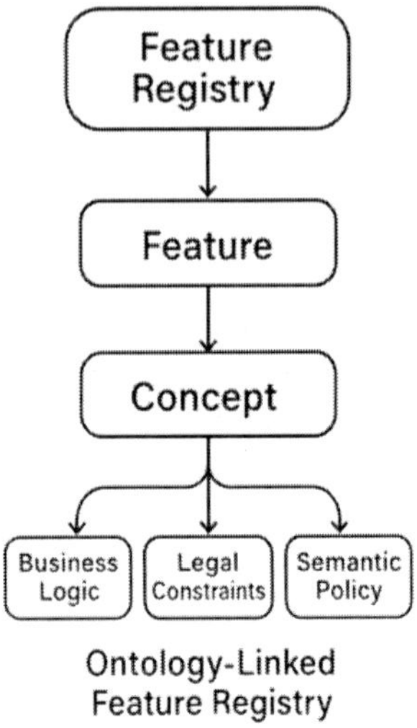

Figure 14.1 Features linked to concepts and policies.

Principle 2: Ontology-Driven Alignment

Semantic contracts act as guardrails for both humans and machines defining not only shape but intention, context, and usage constraints.

Ontology Layers

To resolve mismatched definitions across departments or geographies, a shared ontology provides a controlled vocabulary and relationship model. Terms like "customer activity" or "account age" are bound to canonical concepts that transcend local systems.

Principle 3: Assertions as Preventative Guardrails

Ontologies support cross-system interoperability, align features with business meaning, and provide a foundation for governance, audit, and ML resilience.

Semantic Assertions and Validation

A growing best practice is the use of semantic assertions, business logic embedded in code that asserts preconditions, invariants, and meaning. For example, if a field is labeled "historical," future timestamps should be disallowed. A rules engine can catch violations in staging or even during CI/CD.

Semantic assertions shift validation left ensuring meaning is verified at design time, not post-hoc.

Once meaning is defined, the challenge becomes reinforcement at scale. This is where automation enters, not to replace governance, but to extend it.

Even in highly automated AI pipelines, human-in-the-loop feedback remains essential. Not every semantic flaw or ethical risk can be detected by logic or statistics alone. Domain experts, impacted stakeholders, and governance stewards provide interpretive context that machines lack. By embedding review cycles, escalation paths, and override mechanisms, organizations can flag unanticipated edge cases, detect emergent bias, and reinforce semantic integrity. In this way, human oversight acts as an interpretive safety net, especially when models operate in ambiguous, high-stakes, or evolving environments.

Semantic drift can take many forms; some detectable through statistics, others only through context or governance checks. This radar visual captures six key categories of semantic drift and their relative severity in a given system or model:

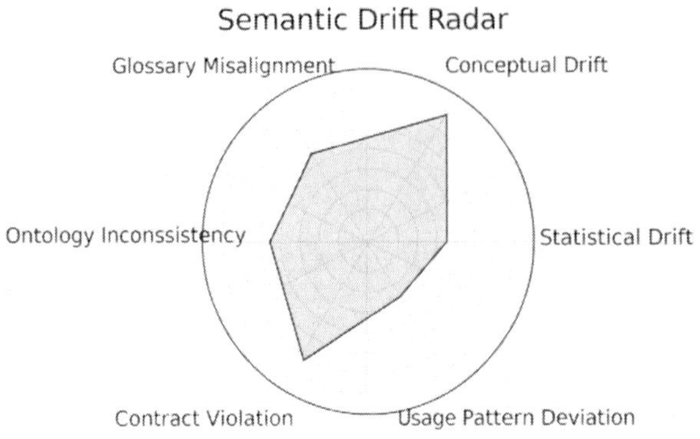

Figure 14.2 Radar of semantic drift dimensions.

Augmenting with AI Agents – Governance at Machine Scale

As governance scaled, the bank embedded AI agents into its MLops stack. These agents:

- Monitored feature importance drift
- Queried semantic registries
- Flagged anomalies
- Recommended corrective actions

These systems extended beyond anomaly detection. They performed context-aware correlation, comparing present values to historical semantics. When the customer_tenure feature's importance spiked, an agent triangulated its history, detected a definitional shift, and recommended model rollback.

Technical Extension: LLMOps and Proactive Monitoring

Explainable AI (XAI) components like SHAP revealed which misaligned features influenced predictions. Agents scanned feature stores and surfaced concept drift before errors reached production.

Integrated into LLMOps workflows, these agents served as semantic sentinels, watching not just for data quality violations but for conceptual contradictions. They enforced meaning-based CI checks, acting as stewards of the organization's collective understanding.

These agents did more than monitor they understood. Context-aware automation is the next frontier of scalable trust.

To operationalize these principles at machine scale, many organizations are deploying AI agents; tools that don't just monitor data, but interpret, align, and govern it automatically. Together, these agents form a layered ecosystem that spans detection, validation, documentation, and alignment. The table below summarizes each role, its primary function, and the organizational outcomes they support:

Agent Role	**Primary Function**	**Outcome**
Drift Watchdogs	Monitor semantic drift in features and models	Prevents silent model failures due to conceptual drift
Glossary Assistants	Suggest and refine term definitions across systems	Keeps business vocabulary aligned and evolving
Contract Auditors	Enforce data contracts and pipeline constraints	Blocks bad data from entering production systems
Lineage Mappers	Trace data lineage and detect undocumented flows	Improves trust and traceability of data transformations

Privacy Sentinels	Ensure privacy compliance and consent enforcement	Reduces regulatory risk from improper data use
Smart Documenters	Auto-generate documentation and metadata	Supports audits and improves onboarding
Ontology Reconcilers	Align and reconcile ontologies across domains	Facilitates cross-domain data interoperability

Revised Conclusion – Designing for Trustworthy AI

In the age of AI, data is no longer just an input. It becomes the worldview of a machine.

That worldview is shaped by how we define, structure, and steward meaning. Without clear semantics, even the most advanced models can amplify confusion. Without ownership, automation breeds entropy. Without cultural fluency, contracts and ontologies remain inert documents, not living systems.

Across this book, we've seen how data work breaks when it's treated as an afterthought and how it thrives when meaning comes first. We've learned that failure doesn't begin with broken tools; it begins with broken understanding.

AI doesn't eliminate the need for human judgment. It elevates the cost of getting it wrong.

Our challenge now is not to simply build smarter systems, but to build more accountable ones. To design pipelines that reflect purpose, features that carry intent, and teams that share a common language. Because what machines learn (and what decisions they make) begins with what we choose to define.

Trustworthy AI doesn't start with the model. It starts with meaning.

Bias Mitigation in Semantic AI Systems

Bias in AI rarely originates from the model itself; it begins in the semantics of the data we choose, the labels we define, and the proxies we accept as signals of behavior. When definitions carry historical prejudice, regional variation, or unexamined assumptions, models learn and amplify those patterns. Effective bias mitigation is therefore not just a statistical correction technique. It is a semantic governance process. It requires clarifying the meaning behind features, validating how concepts are used across contexts, and embedding human-in-the-loop review for decisions that carry ethical weight. In practice, this looks like fairness-aware evaluation sets, demographic performance slices, explanation tooling, and governance workflows that treat accountability as a design property, not an afterthought.

Semantic Clarity as a Guardrail Against AI Bias

Bias in AI systems often originates not in the algorithm, but in the ambiguity of upstream definitions. When fields like "risk score," "household size," or "employment status" lack clear semantics, models encode assumptions that go unexamined introducing hidden bias into high-stakes decisions. Semantic contracts, glossary alignment, and stewardship practices act as ethical guardrails. They surface assumptions, enforce transparency, and enable teams to interrogate not just *how* models perform, but *what* they are learning. In this way, clarity isn't just a technical asset. It's an ethical imperative.

As soon as models begin shaping real outcomes—credit decisions, patient prioritization, hiring filters—semantic clarity becomes not just operational, but ethical.

Ethical Implications of Data Usage and Governance

In the age of AI, ethical considerations around data usage and governance have moved from peripheral concerns to central obligations. As data increasingly informs high-stakes decisions—from healthcare treatments and financial lending to employment opportunities and criminal justice—organizations have a moral responsibility to ensure data is managed ethically, transparently, and fairly.

Bias and Fairness in Data

Ambiguities or biases embedded within semantics can lead to significant ethical pitfalls. Consider scenarios such as biased hiring algorithms or unfair credit scoring systems that inadvertently penalize groups based on gender, race, or other protected attributes. Such issues often stem from biased historical data or semantic definitions that encode hidden assumptions.

Organizations must proactively:

- Identify and mitigate biases in semantic definitions.
- Validate data and model outputs across diverse demographic groups.
- Regularly audit data semantics to detect and correct biases early.

Transparency and Explainability

Ethical data governance demands clarity and transparency. Stakeholders have the right to understand how decisions that affect their lives are made.

Semantic clarity supports this ethical imperative by ensuring data terms, metrics, and models are interpretable.

- Clearly documented semantic contracts help stakeholders comprehend decision logic.
- Explainable AI (XAI) practices leverage semantic governance to interpret model outputs clearly.
- Transparent lineage tracking ensures accountability and builds stakeholder trust.

Data Privacy and Consent

Beyond regulatory compliance, ethical data governance involves genuinely respecting individuals' privacy rights and managing their data with integrity and care. Organizations must handle consent not merely as a checkbox but as an ethical commitment:

- Clearly inform stakeholders how their data will be used.
- Implement robust semantic-driven consent management systems.
- Regularly audit data usage against declared purposes and consent boundaries.

Example: Ethical Governance in Action

A healthcare provider, guided by ethical governance, implemented semantic contracts specifying patient data usage clearly. Beyond meeting HIPAA compliance, they embedded ethics-driven privacy checks ensuring data was only accessible and utilized for consented, transparent purposes. By proactively addressing potential biases in patient data used for predictive models, they reduced unfair disparities in care recommendations.

Guiding Principles for Ethical Data Governance

- **Accountability:** Clearly assign ethical oversight responsibilities within data governance roles.
- **Inclusivity:** Actively incorporate diverse perspectives to uncover and correct potential biases.
- **Transparency:** Maintain open documentation and clear communication of data semantics, uses, and decisions.
- **Respect:** Treat stakeholder data with care, respecting privacy, consent, and intended use.

Embedding these ethical considerations into your governance framework not only protects your organization from reputational and legal risks but also fosters deeper stakeholder trust, ensuring your data practices are not just legally compliant but morally sound.

Closing Reflection: Designing for the Human Future

We began this book by asking why data projects fail. And again and again, the answer was the same: not because we lacked technology, but because we lacked shared meaning. Misaligned definitions, unowned metrics, implicit assumptions. These fractures undermine trust long before a pipeline ever breaks.

But failure is not inevitable.

Success comes from designing data with intention: from aligning teams around language, from embedding meaning into systems, and from treating trust not as an aspiration, but as a deliverable. When meaning is clear, workflows accelerate. When ownership is understood, accountability grows. When data is designed to be interpreted (by people and by machines) confidence scales with complexity.

In the age of AI, this work becomes even more urgent. Models do not invent understanding. They inherit it. Whatever we make ambiguous, they will amplify. The cost of misalignment becomes exponential.

So, our task is not to build faster pipelines or larger models. Our task is to build systems that can be understood, questioned, and evolved. Systems that preserve context as they scale. Systems that remember why they were created, not just how they run.

Meaning is not a constraint—it is a form of power.
Clarity is not overhead—it is the foundation of trust.
And trust is what allows data to become intelligence, not noise.

The future will be shaped by those who treat understanding as infrastructure. Those who design for interpretability. Those who believe that data is not just numbers, but a language we create together.

Because in the end, progress is not measured by how much data we collect, how fast we compute, or how complex our models become but by how clearly we can explain what they mean.

What we make clear, we can trust. What we can trust, we can scale.

About the Author

Bijo Jose is a seasoned data architecture leader with more than 25 years of experience designing enterprise grade data systems that support mission critical operations. His career spans healthcare, finance, insurance, and the public sector, where he has helped organizations transform fragmented and ambiguous data into governed, trustworthy, and strategically usable assets.

Recognized for his expertise in data strategy, semantic modeling, and governance design, Bijo brings a perspective that balances technical depth with organizational practicality. He has led large scale modernization programs, legacy to cloud migrations, metadata first architectures, and the development of AI ready data platforms.

Bijo is known not only for solving complex data challenges, but for reshaping how organizations think about meaning, trust, and accountability in modern data ecosystems. He champions the view that data is a language, not merely an asset. Through his writing and consulting, and advisory work, he helps teams design systems that preserve meaning, reinforce trust, and maintain accountability, especially as AI increasingly influences and automates decision making.

Glossary of Key Terms

Term	Definition
Active Metadata	Metadata that is continuously updated and used by systems to automate lineage tracking, governance, quality checks, and workflows.
AI/ML Lifecycle	The end-to-end process of developing, deploying, and maintaining machine learning systems, including data collection, feature engineering, model training, evaluation, deployment, monitoring, and retraining.
Analytical Data Model	A model optimized for querying and insights rather than operational transactions, usually in star schema or wide-table form.
Analytics Layer	The part of the data stack where metrics are calculated and visualizations are produced. Often implemented through BI tools or semantic layers.
Bias Mitigation	Techniques to detect, quantify, and reduce unwanted bias in ML models, often by rebalancing datasets, adjusting training strategies, or enforcing fairness constraints.
Business Glossary	A curated dictionary of business terms, metric definitions, and shared vocabulary used across the organization.

Canonical Model	A standardized representation of core business entities and relationships, used to eliminate duplication and support interoperability.
CDO (Chief Data Officer)	A senior executive responsible for data strategy, governance, and treating data as an enterprise asset, often accountable for data quality, compliance, and analytics enablement.
Change Data Capture (CDC)	A method for capturing incremental updates from operational systems and replicating them into analytics environments.
CI/CD (Continuous Integration / Continuous Delivery)	Practices and tooling that automate building, testing, and deploying code and configurations frequently and safely.
Column-Level Lineage	Fine-grained tracing of how each individual field is derived, transformed, and used across pipelines and reports.
DAG (Directed Acyclic Graph)	A graph structure that represents dependencies between tasks or jobs in a workflow or data pipeline.
Data Catalog	A searchable inventory of data assets that exposes metadata such as schema, ownership, definitions, and lineage.
Data Contract	A formal agreement between producers and consumers specifying schema, semantics, quality, and change management rules.

Data First	A design philosophy in which meaning, ownership, and usability of data are treated as primary design concerns.
Data Governance	The organizational framework that ensures data is accurate, secure, consistent, and aligned to shared purpose.
Data Lineage	A traceable record of where data originates, how it is transformed, and where it is used.
Data Mesh	A decentralized architecture where domain teams own their data products, supported by shared standards and infrastructure.
Data Model	A structured description of how data entities relate to each other within a system.
Data Product	A dataset, service, or model built with clarity of purpose, defined interfaces, documentation, lifecycle ownership, and SLAs.
Data Steward	The role responsible for maintaining the meaning, quality, and appropriate usage of data within a domain.
Data Transformation Layer	The set of processes (e.g., dbt models) that convert raw operational data into analytics-ready structures.
Dimensional Model	A modeling approach using facts and dimensions optimized for analytics, clarity, and performance.

Distributed Ownership	A governance model in which responsibility for data meaning and quality resides with the teams closest to it.
DMBOK (Data Management Body of Knowledge)	A comprehensive framework from DAMA International that defines best practices, functions, and principles for managing data as a strategic enterprise asset.
Drift (Concept / Data / Model)	Changes in meaning, distribution, or relationships that degrade validity or interpretation of data or ML models.
DRY (Don't Repeat Yourself)	Define meaning once and reuse it everywhere to prevent semantic drift.
ETL / ELT	Workflows for extracting data, transforming it, and loading it into analytical systems (transform-before-load vs. transform-after-load).
Feature Engineering	The process of selecting, transforming, and creating variables (features) from raw data to improve the performance of ML models. It includes domain expertise and often becomes a bottleneck in model reproducibility.
Feature Store	A centralized system that manages feature definitions, lineage, and reuse across machine learning models.
FHIR (Fast Healthcare Interoperability Resources)	A modern HL7 standard that defines modular "resources" and APIs for exchanging healthcare data electronically

	between systems in a consistent, interoperable way.
GDPR (General Data Protection Regulation)	The EU's comprehensive data protection law that regulates how personal data is collected, processed, stored, and transferred, with strict requirements and significant penalties for non-compliance.
Glossary-Driven Development	Defining key terms and metrics before building dashboards, pipelines, or models to ensure consistency.
HIPAA (Health Insurance Portability and Accountability Act)	A U.S. law that sets standards for protecting the privacy and security of patients' health information and governing how healthcare data can be used and shared.
HL7 (Health Level Seven)	A family of international standards for structuring and exchanging clinical and administrative healthcare data between information systems.
Human-in-the-Loop (HITL)	An approach where human feedback is incorporated into ML workflows for labeling, validation, retraining, or oversight. Essential in LLMOps and high-risk domains to mitigate hallucination, bias, or semantic drift.
ICD (International Classification of Diseases)	A standardized global coding system for diagnoses and health conditions used for reporting and billing

KPI (Key Performance Indicator)	A quantifiable metric used to track progress toward a specific business outcome or objective (e.g., churn rate, conversion rate, on-time delivery).
Lineage Graph	A visual representation of upstream dependencies and downstream consumers of data.
LLMOps (Large Language Model Operations)	An extension of MLOps focused on managing LLMs like GPT or BERT, covering fine-tuning, deployment, monitoring, and governance. It includes safeguards for bias, drift, and hallucination, with emphasis on cost, compliance, and human feedback.
Machine Learning Pipeline	The end-to-end workflow for preparing data, training models, evaluating performance, and deploying predictions.
MDM (Master Data Management)	Maintain authoritative, unified records of core business entities like customers and products.
Minimal Viable Contract (MVC)	The smallest enforceable data agreement needed to prevent breakage while enabling iteration.
MLOps (Machine Learning Operations)	A set of practices that automate and streamline the deployment, monitoring, and governance of machine learning models in production.

OWL (Web Ontology Language)	A formal language designed for representing rich and complex knowledge about things, groups of things, and relations between things. Used in semantic web and AI systems to enable machine-readable logic and inference.
Observability	The ability to assess the health and reliability of data systems using signals like freshness, volume, anomalies, and lineage completeness.
OKR (Objectives and Key Results)	A goal-setting framework that links a qualitative objective to a small set of measurable key results, aligning teams around outcomes rather than activities.
Ontology	A structured representation of concepts and their relationships, enabling shared meaning across systems and teams.
Orchestration	The automated scheduling, execution, and monitoring of data pipelines.
PII (Personally Identifiable Information)	Data that can identify a specific individual (e.g., name, SSN, email, address), either alone or when combined with other data.
SaaS (Software as a Service)	Software delivered over the internet as a subscription service, with the provider managing infrastructure and updates.
Prompt Engineering	The practice of designing and refining input prompts to guide the behavior and output of

	large language models. Prompt engineering is central to effective LLMOps and avoids the need for full retraining.
Provenance	A record of the original source and ownership of data, supporting auditability and trust.
RACI	A responsibility model that clarifies who is Responsible, Accountable, Consulted, and Informed for a given process or decision.
RBAC (Role-Based Access Control)	A method of granting permissions based on a user's role, rather than individual identities.
RDF (Resource Description Framework)	A standard model for data interchange on the web. It structures data as triples (subject-predicate-object) and forms the foundation of the semantic web by enabling linked data and metadata descriptions.
RDM (Reference Data Management)	Govern the codes and categories that classify data so interpretations stay consistent.
SHACL (Shapes Constraint Language)	A standard for validating RDF graphs against schema-like constraints ("shapes"), ensuring semantic integrity of data.
SPARQL	A query language used to retrieve and manipulate RDF data. It enables semantic querying across knowledge graphs and linked data platforms.

Schema Evolution	The controlled process of changing data structure without breaking downstream consumers.
Semantic Drift	A change in meaning that does not alter data structure, often undetected but highly impactful.
Semantic Layer	A business-logic abstraction that provides consistent metric definitions across tools and interfaces.
SLA (Service Level Agreement)	A formal agreement that defines the expected level of service (e.g., uptime, response time, data freshness) and the consequences or remedies if those targets are not met.
Stewardship Model	Defines how data meaning, quality, ownership, and change control are shared or delegated across teams.
Trust Signal	Any indicator (e.g., tests, certifications, adoption metrics) that builds user confidence in a data product.
Versioned Metric	A metric definition tracked across versions to maintain historical accuracy as logic evolves.